Walk Around

F-117A Nighthawk

By James Goodall
Color by Don Greer
Illustrated by Richard Hudson and Ernesto Cumpian

Walk Around Number 26

squadron/signal publications

Introduction

My involvement with 'black' (secret) aircraft goes back to 10 March 1964. This was the day I was up-close-and-personal with my very first Blackbird, a Lockheed/Air Force YF-12A, tail number 06934. That encounter was all it took to hook me for life.

Twenty-five years later, I saw my first **F-117 Nighthawk**. I first heard reference to what is now known as HAVE BLUE (the technology demonstrator for the F-117) in early 1977. This was months before the first airframe was assembled and later delivered to Area 51, the place in the Nevada desert that 'does not exist.' Until the formal announcement of the F-117A on 10 November 1988, all I had to work from was pure speculation on what – if anything – was going on in the desert north of Las Vegas. The description we had of the F-117 was like the old story of a blind man describing an elephant: All the various parts were right, just not in the proper order.

The formal public unveiling of the F-117 program took place on 21 April 1990, but the world would have to wait until the night of 16/17 January 1991 to really see the F-117A in action. Much to the surprise of Iraqi leader Saddam Hussein, his heavily defended city of Baghdad was no match for the US Air Force's wing of F-117A stealth fighters. The 'Black Jet' flew 1261 sorties over Baghdad and came out without a scratch – not bad for the 'ugliest' aircraft in the world!

My numerous requests over the years for close-up access to the F-117A have all been denied. The Air Force still enforces its 20-foot (6.1 м) rule: No one but authorized personnel are allowed to get any closer. With that restriction in mind, I want to thank some of the many people without whose cooperation this book would still be a dream. These include the very cooperative and accommodating Public Affairs staff at the US Air Force Museum. This also includes the management and staff at the Lockheed Martin Skunk Works, including the late Ben R. Rich, Jack Gordon, Paul Martin, Bill Fox, Bob Murphy, Denny Lombard, and the late Bill Park, to name but a few. I also thank the original Lockheed/Air Force flight test and evaluation team at Area 51 and the members of the 4450th Tactical Group and its successor, the 37th Tactical Fighter Wing. My deep appreciation goes to those brave men and women who fought and flew in Operation DESERT STORM. In this new century, I was greatly assisted by the current operators of the Nighthawk, the men and women of the 49th Fighter Wing stationed at Holloman Air Force Base, New Mexico. The list of thanks includes my dearest friend, the late John Andrews; one of the best photo shooters today, Tony Landis; Brian 'Buck' Rogers; Greg L. Davis; Chris Mayer; Chuck Mayer, and the very talented Jay Miller. I also thank my very first co-author, Bill Sweetman; Stuart Brown, formerly with Popular Science and now at Fortune Magazine; Paul Crickmore; Tom Tulus; and Doug Slowiak. Thanks also go to Kevin Patrick; Marty Isham; Kevin Helm (you must visit Kevin's website at http://www.f-117a.com); Harold Helm; the late Nick Waters; and former F-117 pilot Steve 'Buck' Paulson. I must also credit all of the original Groom Lake Interceptors: Glenn Campbell (not the singer!); Tom Mahood; the infamous John Lear; two of Tulare's finest cops, Chief Roger Hill and Commander Tom Latrell; the Swiss Mountain Bat; Zero; and Mike Dornheim with AvWeek. My special thanks go to the management and staff at Squadron/Signal for giving me this outlet for my passions. Last, but certainly not least, I thank my beautiful, delightful and wonderful wife, Nora Diane Goodall, for her patience, love, understanding, and invaluable help with this book.

Dedication:

This book would not be a reality if it were not for my dearest friend, 'Mr. Testors' – or as Ben Rich fondly referred to him, 'that Son of a Bitch from Testors' – John Andrews. The modeling industry lost its best and brightest contributor with John's passing in April of 1999.

John Andrews, Tony Landis, and I were the first civilians to see and photograph the F-117 in its natural habitat in early 1989. It was absolutely exhilarating to stand at the fence line of the Tonopah Test Range, surrounded by ASI security forces and Lincoln County's finest, our cameras in hand, defying the powers that be. Their intent was to harass us out of the area and deny us our chance to see and photograph the as-yet-to-be-seen F-117A. They failed.

Without John's friendship, terrific sense of humor, and the fact that he was one of the best good-guy 'spies' in the business, my interest in black aircraft would never have grown to be what it is today. The net result of his generosity, unwavering loyalty and dedication to his passion – 'black' programs – is evident in the pages of this book.

ISBN 0-89747-425-2

If you have any photographs of aircraft, armor, soldiers or ships of any nation, particularly wartime snapshots, why not share them with us and help make Squadron/Signal's books all the more interesting and complete in the future. Any photograph sent to us will be copied and the original returned. The donor will be fully credited for any photos used. Please send them to:

Squadron/Signal Publications, Inc.
1115 Crowley Drive
Carrollton, TX 75011-5010

Если у вас есть фотографии самолётов, вооружения, солдат или кораблей любой страны, особенно, снимки времён войны, поделитесь с нами и помогите сделать новые книги издательства Эскадрон/Сигнал ещё интереснее. Мы переснимем ваши фотографии и вернём оригиналы. Имена приславших снимки будут сопровождать все опубликованные фотографии. Пожалуйста, присылайте фотографии по адресу:

Squadron/Signal Publications, Inc.
1115 Crowley Drive
Carrollton, TX 75011-5010

軍用機、装甲車両、兵士、軍艦などの写真を所持しておられる方はいらっしゃいませんか？どの国のものでも結構です。作戦中に撮影されたものが特に良いのです。Squadron/Signal社の出版する刊行物において、このような写真は内容を一層充実し、興味深くすることができます。当方にお送り頂いた写真は、複写の後お返しいたします。出版物中に写真を使用した場合は、必ず提供者のお名前を明記させて頂きます。お写真は下記にご送付ください。

Squadron/Signal Publications, Inc.
1115 Crowley Drive
Carrollton, TX 75011-5010

(Front Cover) This Lockheed F-117A Nighthawk was assigned to the Commander of the 37th Tactical Fighter Wing (TFW) at Tonopah Test Range, Nevada. A 2000 pound (907.2 кG) GBU-27 Laser Guided Bomb is mounted on a trapeze in the F-117A's weapons bay.

(Previous Page) An F-117A Nighthawk (81-10796) approaches the runway at Tonopah Test Range during the spring of 1989. Tonopah's 'Man Camp' below the F-117's tail housed the 2500 Nighthawk flight and ground crew personnel. Aircraft 796 flew 29 combat missions during the 1991 Persian Gulf War (Operation DESERT STORM) and was nicknamed FATAL ATTRACTION. (Lockheed Martin)

(Back Cover) An F-117A assigned to the 37th TFW flies over Baghdad, Iraq during the beginning of Operation DESERT STORM on 17 January 1991. The Nighthawk was the only Coalition aircraft that flew over the heavily defended Iraqi capital throughout the Persian Gulf War.

The US Coast and Geodetic Survey photographed the infamous Area 51 'secret' flight test facility at Groom Dry Lake, Nevada in 1968. The US government continues to refuse to officially acknowledge the existence of the base despite its popularity as the focal point of numerous movies, TV tabloid programs, and publications. The 15,000-foot (4572 M) long main runway crosses over the dry lakebed from southeast to northwest.

In 1954, General Manager of the Lockheed Advanced Development Projects (Skunk Works), Clarence L. 'Kelly' Johnson, convinced the Central Intelligence Agency (CIA) that his firm was best equipped to develop the Cold War's new high-altitude secret spy plane, the Lockheed/CIA U-2. This program required a most out-of-the-way location to conduct flight-testing. Skunk Works' Chief Test Pilot Tony LeVier and Senior Design Engineer Dorsey Kammerer identified Groom Dry Lake during an aerial search in February of 1954. It was undoubtedly the most remote and isolated dry lakebed in the Continental United States. LeVier and Kammerer flew Johnson to the site, only to land and step out onto a four-inch (10.2 CM) layer of dust. Johnson's initial thought was that Groom was too remote; however, after further evaluation, Groom was chosen as the best site and construction began in the late spring of 1954, building what was to become the premiere secret flight test facility in the world.

Area 51's main runway was originally 5600 feet (1706.9 M) in length. During the early 1960s, this runway was first extended to 8500 feet (2590.8 M) and later to 15,000 feet. The runway extension was part of a series of improvement made to Area 51 in support of the Lockheed/CIA A-12 Blackbird, which was developed as a U-2 replacement during this period. The flight test area improvements also included new hangars, billeting, a new operations facility, and a fuel farm.

During the rainy season — which happens once every five to seven years — the normally dry lakebed floods with up to four inches of water. When this occurs, the runoff area became unuseable due to the resulting muck and mud, causing major problems for the flight test program. In the mid-1980s, to circumvent the difficulties associated with flooding, the main runway was lengthened to 27,000 feet (8229.6 M) and the portion of the runway that extended into the runoff area was raised. A separate parallel 15,000-foot runway was added south of the lakebed, just east of the primary runway.

During the early days of Blackbird flight testing (1963-65), a Lockheed technician took advantage of the wet weather and had his picture taken as he floated in a small boat complete with fishing gear and a rubber fish!

It was possible for civilians to observe the secret flight test facility from the top of Whitesides Mountain and from Freedom Ridge until these areas were officially removed from public lands in 1994. Prior to the boundary change, the new runway was observed as being used primarily for non-program aircraft, i.e., employee shuttles and other support flights. (USGS via Jim Goodall)

Workers at the Skunk Works' prototype shop assemble the one-third scale HAVE BLUE/F-117A Radar Cross Section (RCS) mockup. The primary materials used were lumber, plywood, and sheet aluminum, which are adequate for flat or faceted aircraft. The mockup was used to conduct RCS trials in the spring of 1976, which confirmed the stealth quality of this design. (Lockheed Martin via Tony Landis)

The second HAVE BLUE (1002) was painted in overall Light Gray (approximately FS35630) for its test flights. No other markings appeared on this aircraft, which made its first flight on 20 July 1978. This HAVE BLUE made 52 flights before crashing due to an in-flight fire on 11 July 1979. Lt Col Ken Dyson, the test pilot, safely ejected from the aircraft and was recovered without injury. (Lockheed Martin via Tony Landis)

Low-observable coatings were applied over the completed HAVE BLUE RCS mockup. The full-size model was moved in total secrecy to the RCS range at Holloman Air Force Base, New Mexico for verification of the reduced RCS factor. The mockup was mounted upside-down on a 40-foot (12.2 M) pole to reduce interference with the radar waves. (Lockheed Martin via Tony Landis)

The undersurface of HAVE BLUE 1002 was flat, with no protrusions to increase the aircraft's radar signature. The elevons positioned inboard on the wings' trailing edges combined the functions of both elevators and ailerons. The HAVE BLUE's overall light gray paint scheme became mottled with use. (Lockheed Martin via Tony Landis)

4

Lockheed XST HAVE BLUE

Light Gray Finish (approximately FS35630).

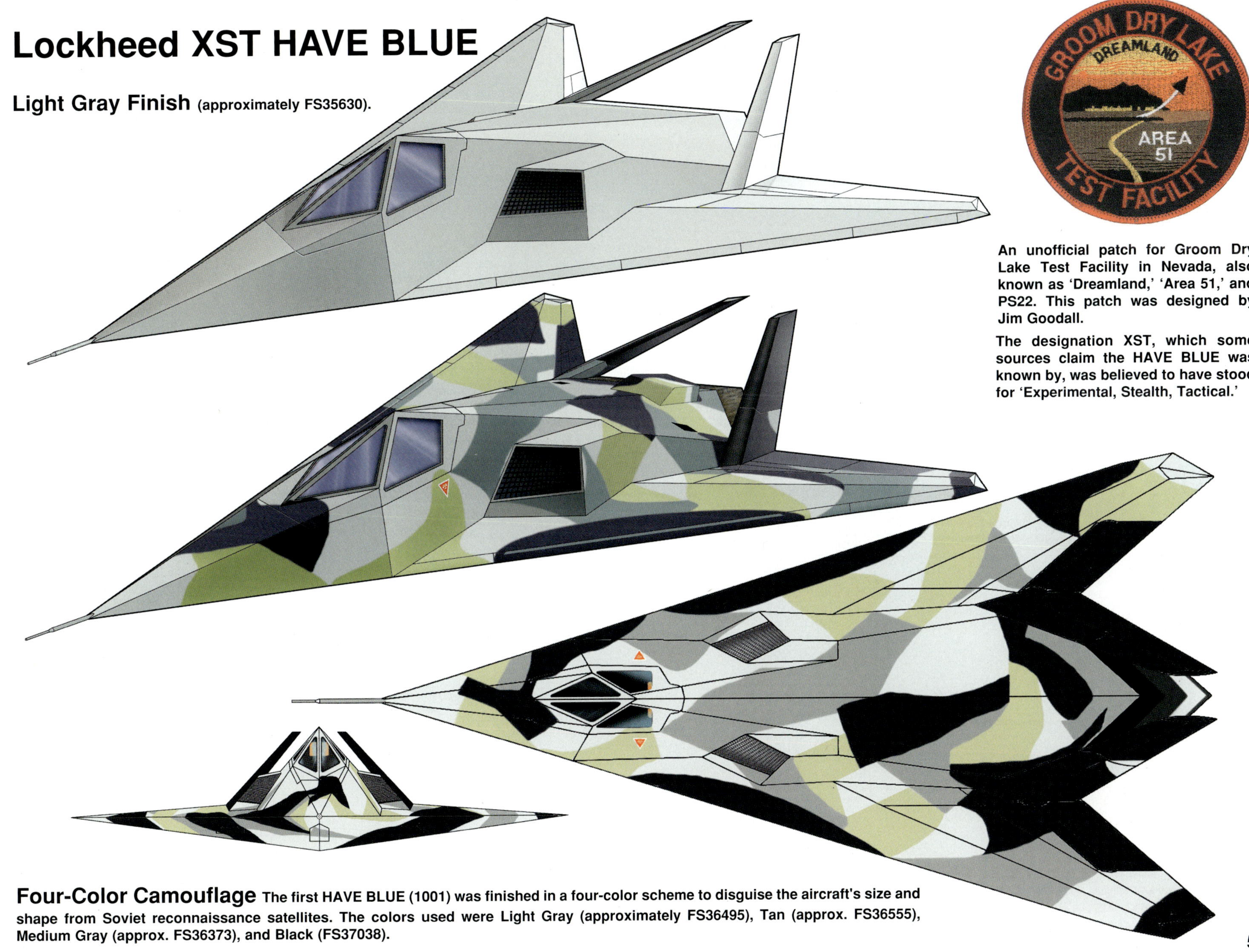

An unofficial patch for Groom Dry Lake Test Facility in Nevada, also known as 'Dreamland,' 'Area 51,' and PS22. This patch was designed by Jim Goodall.

The designation XST, which some sources claim the HAVE BLUE was known by, was believed to have stood for 'Experimental, Stealth, Tactical.'

Four-Color Camouflage The first HAVE BLUE (1001) was finished in a four-color scheme to disguise the aircraft's size and shape from Soviet reconnaissance satellites. The colors used were Light Gray (approximately FS36495), Tan (approx. FS36555), Medium Gray (approx. FS36373), and Black (FS37038).

The F-117A Nighthawk – also dubbed the 'Black Jet' and the 'Cockroach' – was the latest product of the Lockheed Advanced Development Projects company, now the Lockheed Martin Skunk Works. The U-2R (right background) was the last major production model of this high-altitude reconnaissance aircraft. The SR-71A Blackbird (left background) remains the fastest and highest flying air-breathing aircraft ever built. It wouldn't seem possible to have multiple aircraft designed by the same group that would be more different from one another than these three. The F-117A, U-2, and SR-71 were all finished in overall Flat Black (FS37038). (Lockheed Martin)

Ben Rich, president of Lockheed Advanced Development Projects (the Skunk Works), is kneeling in front of his brainchild, the first F-117A operational stealth fighter. Rich – one of the aviation industry's genuine gentlemen – was well known for always making time to interact with fans of these fascinating machines.

By the time of the HAVE BLUE and SENIOR TREND programs which led to the F-117 Nighthawk, Clarence L. 'Kelly' Johnson had been retired from Lockheed for several years. Rich went to the Air Force when Johnson was hospitalized and was not expected to live much longer and requested special permission do a good deed. Rich arranged for a secure TV/VCR (television/video cassette recorder) to be moved right into Johnson's hospital room so he could share a video of the F-117A with the former corporate leader.

It was said that during the design and construction of the A-12 Blackbird strategic reconnaissance aircraft (forerunner of the SR-71), Johnson had so little trust in electronics that he would have invented a hydraulic radio had it been possible! With that thought in mind, as Rich ran the video of his faceted and homely 'Black Jet,' he explained to Johnson that this was not only a 100% fly-by-wire aircraft, but it had been designed with the aid of new software developed by electrical engineers. Johnson, who preferred the use of conventional drawing boards, responded in jest, *"You aren't building that ugly thing in my Skunk Works, are you?"* (Lockheed Martin)

Insignia of the Lockheed Martin Skunk Works, formerly Lockheed's Advanced Development Projects division.

The first HAVE BLUE (1001) is fully assembled in Building 82 of the Lockheed Skunk Works facility in Burbank, California. Red covers protected the engine intakes from ingesting foreign objects and the wing's leading edge from damage to the Radar Absorbent Materials (RAM) on its surface. HAVE BLUE 1001 was later dismantled and flown on a Lockheed C-5A Galaxy to Area 51, where the HAVE BLUE was reassembled and began test flights in December of 1977. (Lockheed Martin via Tony Landis)

A HAVE BLUE is assembled in Building 82 at the Skunk Works in Burbank. Two technicians working beside the port wing leading edge demonstrate the small size of this aircraft. Once the HAVE BLUE was completed, it was disassembled for flight by a C-5A from Burbank to Groom Dry Lake (Area 51) for flight testing. (Lockheed Martin)

HAVE BLUE 1001 is parked in front of Hangar 13 at the south end of the Groom Dry Lake test facility. The aircraft was painted in a disruptive camouflage scheme of light gray, tan, medium gray, and black to disguise its appearance from Soviet reconnaissance satellites. The instrumentation boom on the nose collected static pressure to confirm flight control data. The Lockheed technician sitting in the HAVE BLUE's cockpit lent scale to this aircraft. (Lockheed Martin)

This Lockheed developed three-view drawing demonstrates the HAVE BLUE's configuration. The wings were swept back at 72.5°, in contrast to the 67.5° wing sweep angle of the prototype and production F-117As. The HAVE BLUE's correct dimensions were: 47 feet 3 inches (14.4 M) long, a wingspan of 22 feet 6 inches (6.9 M), and a height of 7 feet 6 inches (2.3 M). (Lockheed Martin)

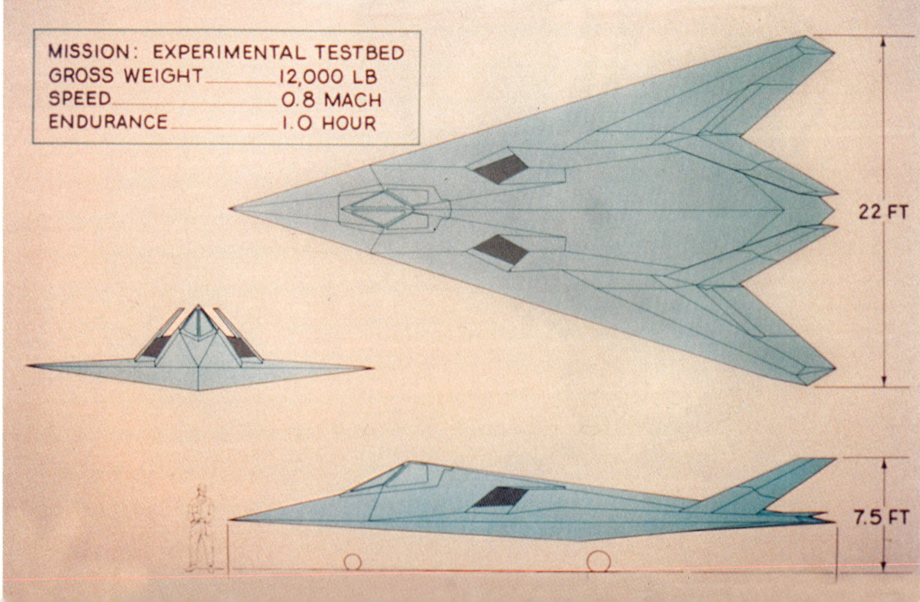

The first YF-117A (79-10780) is assembled shortly after its arrival at Area 51. The aircraft was shown inside Hangar 14 at the south end of the test site (which previously housed the fleet of Lockheed/CIA OXCART A-12 Blackbirds), and was moved from Burbank to Area 51 via a C-5A Galaxy. Red covers protected the leading edges of the wings from damage during aircraft assembly. (Lockheed Martin)

Both exhaust ejector 'platypuses' (shrouds) were removed from this YF-117A at Area 51. This allowed access to the exhaust ducting behind the two General Electric F404 engines. The two weapons bay doors were also opened while technicians examined the Nighthawk. The netting used in place of the hangar doors allowed air circulation on hot desert days, while still providing a visual barrier to the curious eye. (Lockheed Martin)

Red inlet covers, canopy cover, and flight test pitot boom cover were installed on the first YF-117A (780) at Area 51. These covers protected sensitive areas of the airframe while the aircraft was on the ground between flights. Red REMOVE BEFORE FLIGHT flags were attached to the four static pitot tubes on the YF-117A's nose. (Lockheed Martin via Tony Landis)

The panel immediately forward of the YF-117A's cockpit – which housed the Forward Looking Infra-Red (FLIR) unit on production Nighthawks – held avionics equipment. Holes in this panel allowed cooling air to enter this compartment. The gray hose running into the nose landing gear bay provided cooling air for this area during maintenance. (Lockheed Martin via Tony Landis)

The F-117A is equipped with four static pitot tubes on her nose. One tube is mounted in the center, two are placed to starboard, and the other is mounted to port. These probes collect air pressure, temperature, and humidity. This data is fed into the F-117A's fly-by-wire flight control system, which has quadruple redundancy in the event of a system failure. (Jim Goodall)

The two pitot tubes mounted on the F-117A's starboard nose are projected on wedges, which allow the probes to face into the airstream. The port tube is also mounted on a wedge, while the center probe was placed directly on the aircraft's centerline. The panel on the starboard nose undersurface houses the Nighthawk's Downward Looking Infra-Red (DLIR) sensor. (Jim Goodall)

The F-117A's four pitot tubes were made of special plastic materials developed by Lockheed to reduce radar reflectivity. Most aircraft pitot tubes were built from stainless steel and nickel, which reflect radar waves. The Nighthawk's probes can be heated to 1000° F (537.8° C) to boil off and remove any moisture and water built-up at altitude, which interfered with data readings. (Jim Goodall)

Each of the pitot tube's four facets contain a single orifice for air data collection. The port and starboard orifices collected differential pressure to determine the aircraft's angle of sideslip (deviation from the correct flightpath). The upper and lower openings collected differential pressure to determine the angle of attack. The two openings along the probe's side aft of the tip took static pressure measurements. (Jim Goodall)

The F-117A's pitot tubes – like the rest of the aircraft – were designed and built to produce a miniscule Radar Cross Section (RCS) over those fitted to conventional aircraft. The Nighthawk's external surfaces were faceted to discourage radar returns to enemy receivers. Most F-117A external surfaces were swept at least 30° from the vertical to maximize radar energy deflection. (Jim Goodall)

The four pitot tubes provided the only protrusion to the F-117A's nose. The aircraft's panels and doors were designed to help reduce the Nighthawk's RCS when either closed or opened. The DLIR was positioned aft of the nose probes, next to the nose landing gear doors. This pedestal-mounted YF-117A prototype (79-10780) serves as a gate guard at Nellis Air Force Base (AFB), Nevada. (Jim Goodall)

The top secret Low Observable (LO) coatings were removed from this YF-117A (79-10781) prior to this aircraft being put on display at the US Air Force Museum at Wright-Patterson AFB, Ohio. The Nighthawk's nose-mounted static probes were made from a Lockheed-developed heat-resistant plastic, which was also a Radar Absorbent Material (RAM). The Museum's aircraft also lacks the special leading and trailing edges used on the actual aircraft. (Tom Tulus)

The first SENIOR TREND YF-117A (79-10780) made its initial flight on 18 June 1981. The four-color Israeli-style camouflage hid the aircraft's shape from Soviet spy satellites during daylight operations. The YF-117A was fitted with a flight test pitot boom on the nose and the small twin vertical tail surfaces. The latter were enlarged on production F-117As. The number 780 on the tail was black. (Lockheed Martin)

Early flight-test YF-117As were painted in a distinct four-color finish, without national markings. The author once asked the Skunk Works' Ben Rich why the F-117A was painted all black versus the four-color scheme or even medium gray. His answer was: *"The Golden Rule – those that have the gold, rule."* The Air Force wanted the F-117 painted black to benefit the nighttime missions planned for this aircraft. (Lockheed Martin via Tony Landis)

Lockheed test pilot Hal Farley begins his egress from YF-117A Number 780 (nicknamed 'Scorpion 1') after the aircraft's first flight on 18 June 1981. Two company technicians await Farley's departure from the SENIOR TREND. The Low Observable (LO) saw-tooth modifications to the canopy were not yet made at the time of the first flight. (Lockheed Martin via Tony Landis)

Hal Farley poses before the YF-117A after his first flight in the SENIOR TREND on 18 June 1981. This initial flight took place almost one year later than originally planned, due to technical difficulties. The YF-117A's tail number sequence began with 780 because the first flight was to have occurred during July (the seventh month) of 1980. (Lockheed Martin)

A tug moves the fuselage assembly of the first YF-117 (79-10780) down Lockheed's Burbank, California production line. This author was told that early on during the assembly of 780's fuselage, a tug bumped the assembly fixture. This seemingly insignificant contact moved the fixture and resulted in an asymmetrical aircraft. The problem was not discovered until the General Electric engines were being installed in both bays: one engine fit, but the other didn't. (Lockheed Martin)

The first YF-117A fuselage assembly is moved down the production line at Burbank, where the wing assemblies await attachment to the fuselage. A tractor towed the assembly fixture carrying the fuselage to the next stage of assembly. Portions of the wing and fuselage assemblies were temporarily covered to protect the Radar Absorbent Materials (RAM) applied to these surfaces. (Lockheed Martin)

Lockheed technicians prepare to attach the wings to the fuselage and perform other tasks at this factory station. Light green work platforms beside the aircraft will be placed over the wings once the wings and fuselage have been mated. These platforms allowed workers to install the YF-117A's nose, control systems, and engines. (Lockheed Martin)

Construction of the YF-117 prototypes and F-117A production aircraft occurred at Lockheed's Burbank plant. Technicians attached the fuel lines, wire harnesses, and control cables to aircraft 780, after the wings (covered by work platforms) were attached to the fuselage. The ailerons were then installed onto the wings and a function test was performed on all aircraft systems. (Lockheed Martin)

The FLIR system's ball turret consists of three separate elements: the narrow-field-of-view camera, the large zoom camera, and the laser designator. These elements allow the pilot to navigate, find his target, and designate the weapons. The two white tubes protruding immediately aft of the F-117A's cockpit are the aircraft's localizer antennas, which receive radio beams to assist the pilot in instrument ('blind') landings. (Jim Goodall)

The mesh screen in front of the FLIR assembly is reflective to radar. This screen appears to be a solid surface at first glance; however, the FLIR unit can see through this mesh. Radar cannot penetrate the round turret or the camera windows, assisting the F-117A's 'stealthiness.' The FLIR head turned 80° to the closed position when not in use to protect the sensitive optical surface. (Jim Goodall)

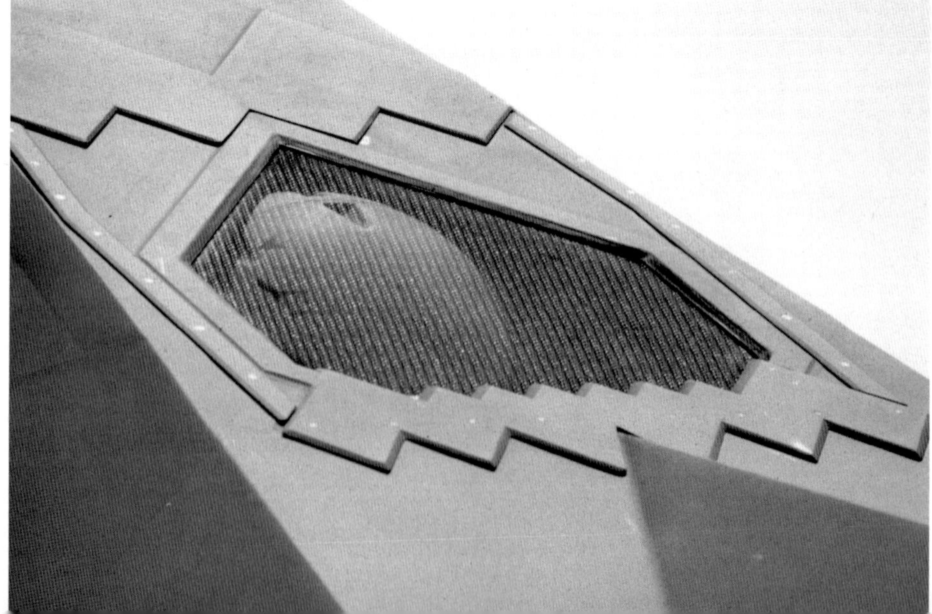

The F-117's FLIR (Forward Looking Infra-Red) turret was mounted immediately forward of the aircraft's windshield. The FLIR and the DLIR (Downward Looking Infra-Red) turret under the nose were part of the Texas Instruments (TI) IRADS (Infra-Red Acquisition and Detection System). This Nighthawk was retrofitted with the TI F3 FLIR turret after DESERT STORM in 1991. The F3 features a larger and more powerful turret assembly than the earlier FLIR unit fitted to F-117As. The laser designator unit is mounted beside the larger IR unit in the FLIR turret. (Paul Crickmore)

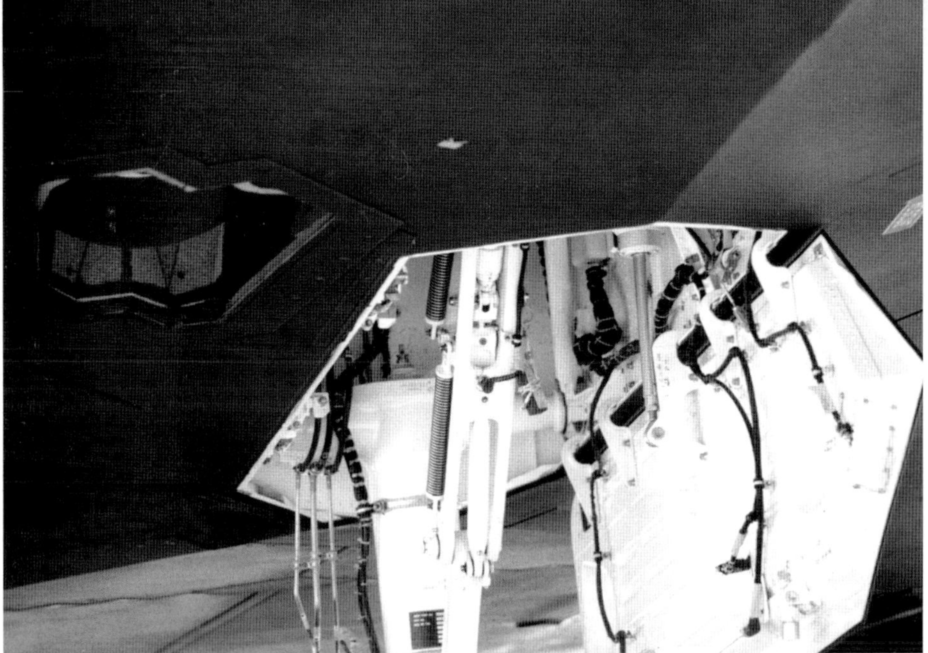

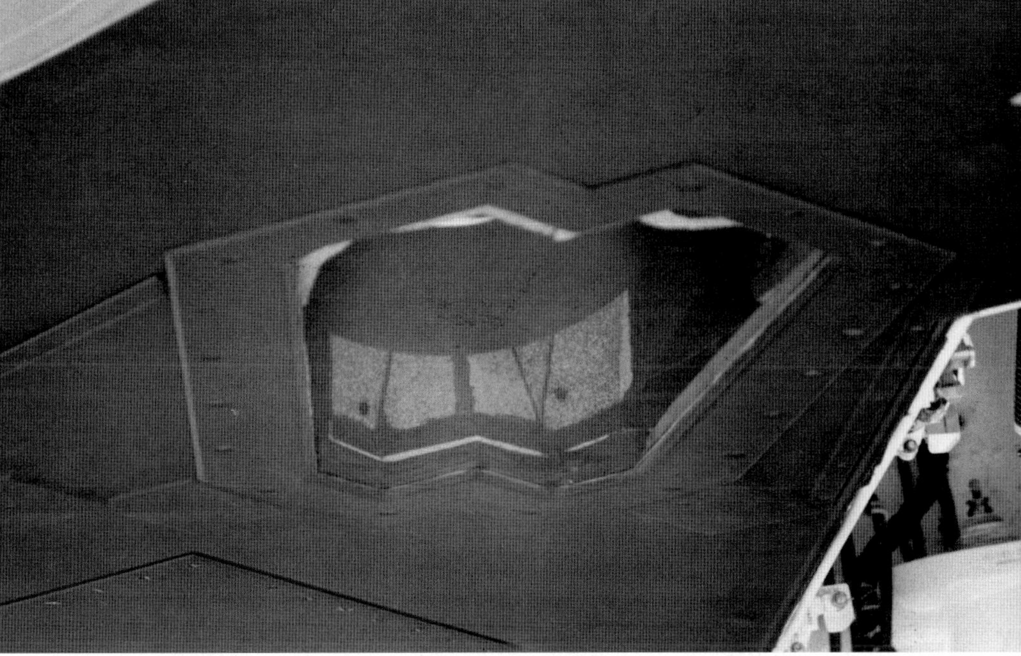

The F-117A's DLIR (Downward Looking Infra-Red) unit was mounted immediately starboard of the nose landing gear well. The DLIR turret, like that the of FLIR in the upper nose, provided the Nighthawk's pilot with search and target acquisition information and target designation. All wiring and associated cables are black, while the gear bay, door interior, and struts are Gloss White (FS17875). (Jim Goodall)

TI's DLIR is positioned to the right of the F-117A's nose wheel assembly. Like with the FLIR, the DLIR is protected by a fine mesh screen, which deflects radar waves from the turret. The saw-toothed and faceted DLIR assembly frame also deflects radar waves. Air Force restrictions prevent civilians from getting closer than 20 feet (6.1 M) to the F-117A; thus, I was not allowed to photograph the Nighthawk's underside. (Jim Goodall)

The F-117A uses the DLIR in conjunction with the FLIR to locate, 'laze' (laser designate), and hit the target – at night, from an altitude of 25,000 feet (7620 M)! The combination of these two systems is called the Infra-Red Acquisition and Designation (IRAD) system. The DLIR's ball turret is identical to that used with the FLIR. During a bombing run, the IRAD looks at the target through both the FLIR and the DLIR. When the F-117A passes a point where the FLIR can no longer acquire and track the target, the IRAD seamlessly transfers the image from the FLIR to the DLIR. (Jim Goodall)

DLIR

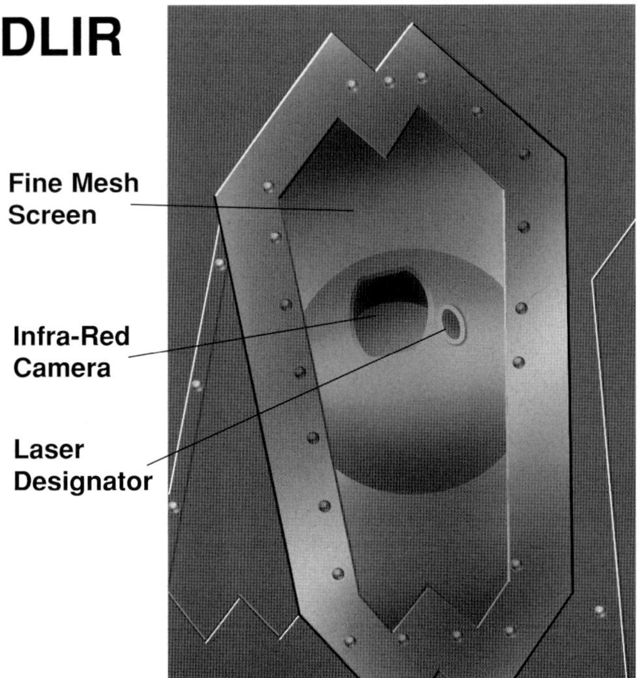

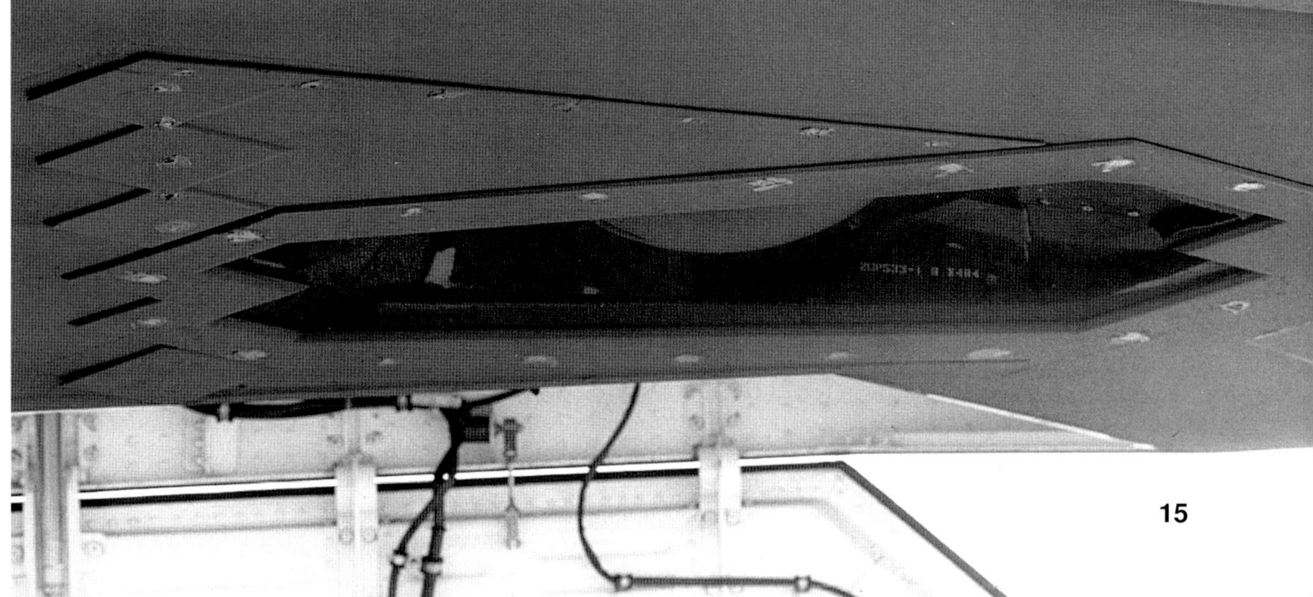

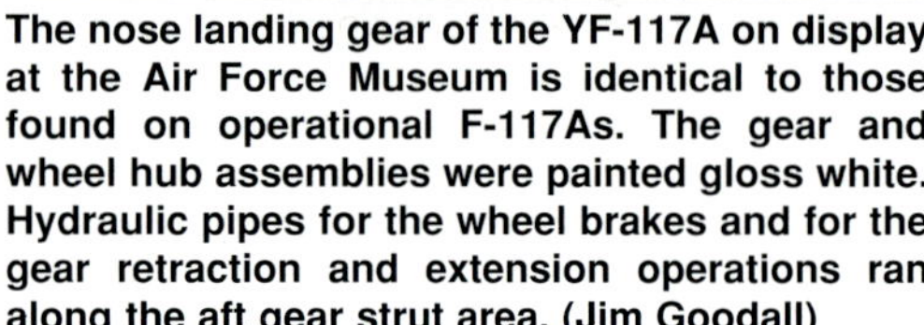

The nose landing gear of the YF-117A on display at the Air Force Museum is identical to those found on operational F-117As. The gear and wheel hub assemblies were painted gloss white. Hydraulic pipes for the wheel brakes and for the gear retraction and extension operations ran along the aft gear strut area. (Jim Goodall)

The nose landing gear was covered when retracted by a single gear door hinged to port. This door's saw-toothed edges reflected radar waves away from the aircraft. The retraction strut pulled the landing gear main strut up and into the gear bay. The Goodyear tire's brand mark was painted white for this airshow appearance; this mark is normally left in the natural tire color while the aircraft is in service. (Jim Goodall)

The nose landing gear steering assembly was mounted to starboard of the main gear strut. Associated plumbing and wiring runs from inside the gear bay down into the top of this assembly. The pilot selected nosewheel steering while the aircraft was taxiing, at the beginning of take off, and shortly after landing. (Jim Goodall)

The Goodyear nose landing gear tire measures 22 inches (55.9 CM) in diameter by 6.6 to 10 inches (16.8 to 25.4 CM) wide. Most F-117As have the three-digit tail number painted in red or black on the nose wheel carry-through assembly. This number is derived from the last three numbers of the aircraft's serial number; for example, 781's full serial is 79-10781. (Jim Goodall)

The nose landing gear retracted upward and forward into the landing gear bay. This system allowed the gear to manually extend downward in the event of hydraulic system failure. The single gear door is hinged to port and is supplied with a separate hydraulic unit to ensure a tight fit upon closing. The bay was painted Gloss White (FS17875), which allowed for easier detection of leaking hydraulic liquid by maintenance crews. The associated boxes and panels inside the nose gear bay are painted black. These boxes include electrical sources for the nose gear-mounted landing light and hydraulic pumps for the brake and gear operation systems. A natural metal air temperature sensor is mounted forward of the landing gear bay. (Jim Goodall)

The forward section of the nose landing gear bay is devoid of equipment to allow room for the retracted nose gear tire and wheel assembly. A bulge in the gear door interior allowed the gear tire to fit entirely inside the bay when retracted. The screw heads inside the bay are painted either red or gray as a measure against corrosion. (Jim Goodall)

The Nighthawk's canopy is raised to allow good forward and side visibility for the pilot. The FLIR (Forward Looking Infra-Red) turret is mounted immediately forward of the windshield to provide forward target acquisition and guidance under all lighting conditions. Flight data collected by the four pitot tubes was fed to the F-117A's fly-by-wire flight control system. (Jim Goodall)

A rearward facing light is mounted at the top of the F-117A's canopy. This light is used for nighttime mid-air refueling operations and illuminates the air refueling receptacle mounted on the upper mid-fuselage. (Tony Landis)

The air refueling light is faceted like the rest of the F-117A's external surface to deflect radar returns from the aircraft. This white light source allows tanker boom operators to clearly find the refueling receptacle at night. (Tony Landis)

The F-117A's windshield was incorporated into the canopy, which was faceted to match the nose and forward fuselage contours. The engine intakes flank the cockpit area, with intake suction relief doors mounted immediately aft of the intakes. Two flush Automatic Direction Finder (ADF) antennas are fitted immediately aft of the canopy to receive radio signals from ground stations. These signals were relayed to the ADF, aiding the pilot in navigation along a flight route. (Lockheed Martin)

The F-117A canopy is a heavy one-piece, all-metal unit with five clear panels of optically pure polycarbonate (plastic). The clear panels are specially coated with gold film to lower radar returns from the cockpit. All canopy panel edges have a saw-tooth design and the edges of the individual saw-tooth surfaces are also faceted to deflect radar waves. (Jim Goodall)

A Head-Up Display (HUD) mounted atop the F-117A's instrument shroud displays flight and target information to the pilot at his eye level. The black instrument shroud protects the rear of the aircraft's instruments from Foreign Object Damage (FOD). This Nighthawk lacks the standard instrument panel glare shields flanking the HUD, which are installed on all operational F-117As. (Jim Goodall)

The Nighthawk's canopy is held in place by six robust attachment pins: three on each side. Two hydraulic screw jacks lift the aft-hinged canopy assembly, which is jettisoned immediately before ejection in an emergency. The canopy interior structure is Flat Black (FS37038) to reduce cockpit glare. The F-117A has a large cockpit from the shoulders down; however, the tapered shape of the canopy allows little room for the pilot's head and helmet. (Jim Goodall)

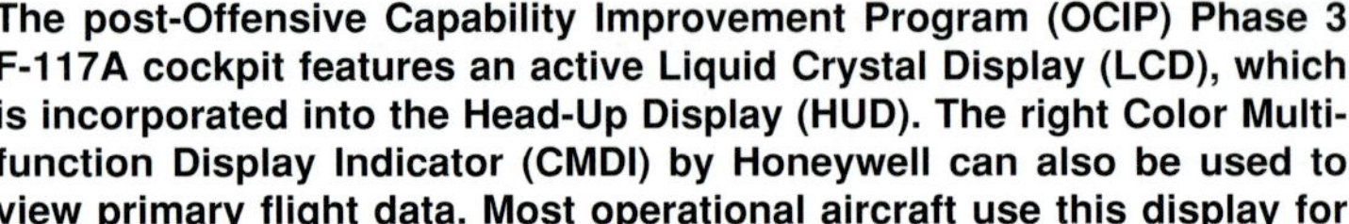

The post-Offensive Capability Improvement Program (OCIP) Phase 3 F-117A cockpit features an active Liquid Crystal Display (LCD), which is incorporated into the Head-Up Display (HUD). The right Color Multi-function Display Indicator (CMDI) by Honeywell can also be used to view primary flight data. Most operational aircraft use this display for the Horizontal Situation Indicator (HSI), moving map, or access to air-craft maintenance status pages. When the pilot selects the attack mode on the HUD, the display automatically cues the weapons arming page. Function keys surround the two CMDIs, allowing the pilot to call up the required display mode. (Lockheed Martin)

This patch was worn by personnel of the F-117A Depot Modification Center – also called PS77 – in Palmdale, California. The last digit in PS77 was missing on this par-ticular patch. This facility per-forms airframe and avionics mod-ifications on Nighthawks.

The Scorpion Flight Test patch was authorized for personnel assigned to the F-117A flight test program at Groom Dry Lake.

The five YF-117A SENIOR TREND prototypes used analog (conventional) flight instruments in place of the CMDIs and IRAD (Infra-Red Acquisition and Designation) system displays installed on production Nighthawks. The artificial horizon – the light blue and black sphere – was placed in the panel's center. Some test instruments were removed from the cockpit of this YF-117A on display at the US Air Force Museum. (Jim Goodall)

The starboard side of the YF-117A's instrument panel is the same as for operational F-117As, along with the control stick and the lower center instrument display immediately forward of the stick. Controls for the aircraft's radio and intercom systems were placed on the lower center display. The remainder of the YF-117A cockpit differed in composition from those found in the production Nighthawks. (Jim Goodall)

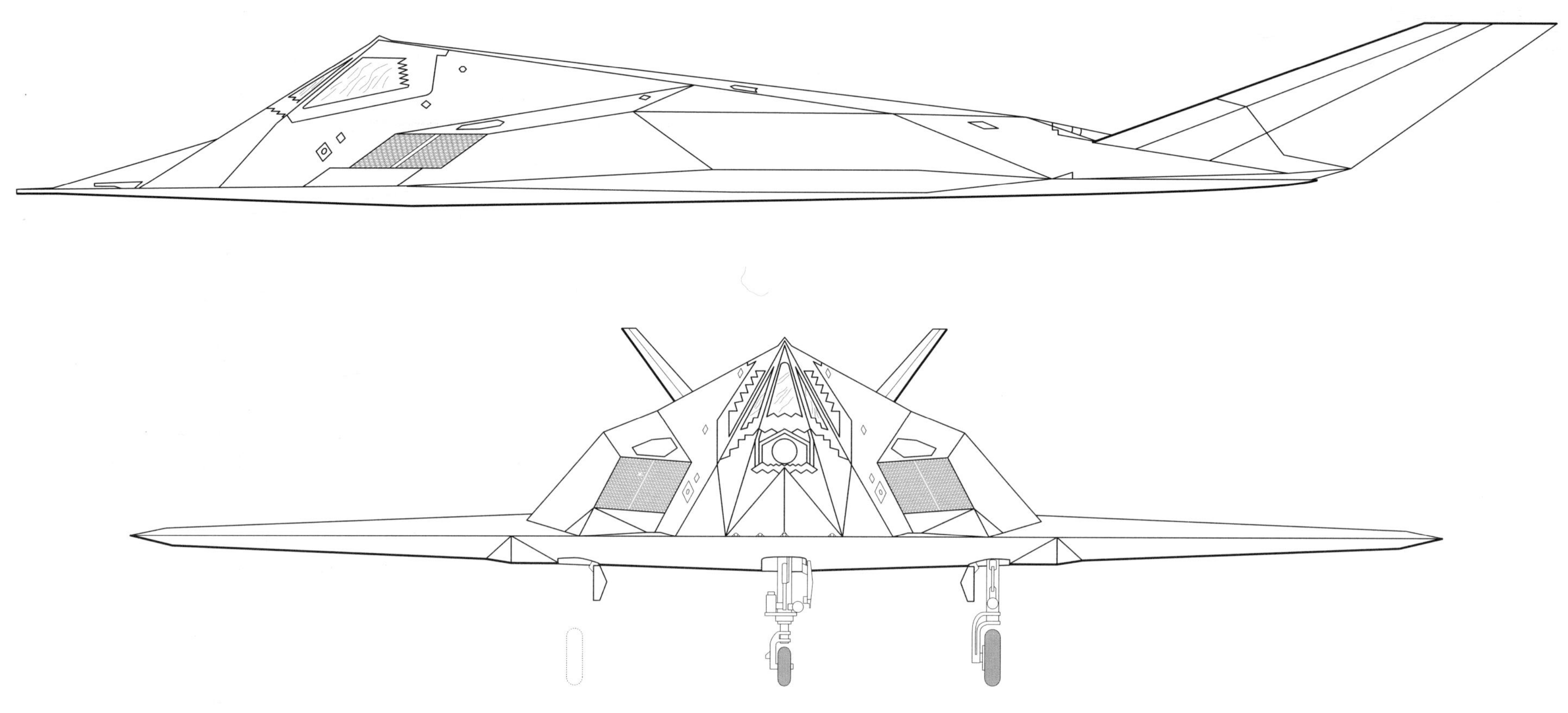

Lockheed Martin F-117A Nighthawk Specifications

Wingspan................43 feet 4 inches (13.2 M)
Length.....................65 feet 11 inches (20.1 M)
Height.....................12 feet 5 inches (3.8 M)
Empty Weight..........29,500 pounds (13,381.2 KG)
Maximum Weight....52,500 pounds (23,814 KG)
Powerplant...............Two 10,800 pound thrust General Electric
              F404-GE-F1D2 low bypass turbofan engines

Armament.................Two 2000 pound (907.2 KG) laser guided bombs or
              other guided weapons
Maximum Speed......603 MPH (970.4 KMH) at 35,000 feet (10,668 M)
Service Ceiling.........52,000 feet (15,849.6 M)
Maximum Range......1250 miles (2011.6 KM) on internal fuel; unlimited
              with aerial refueling
Crew..........................One

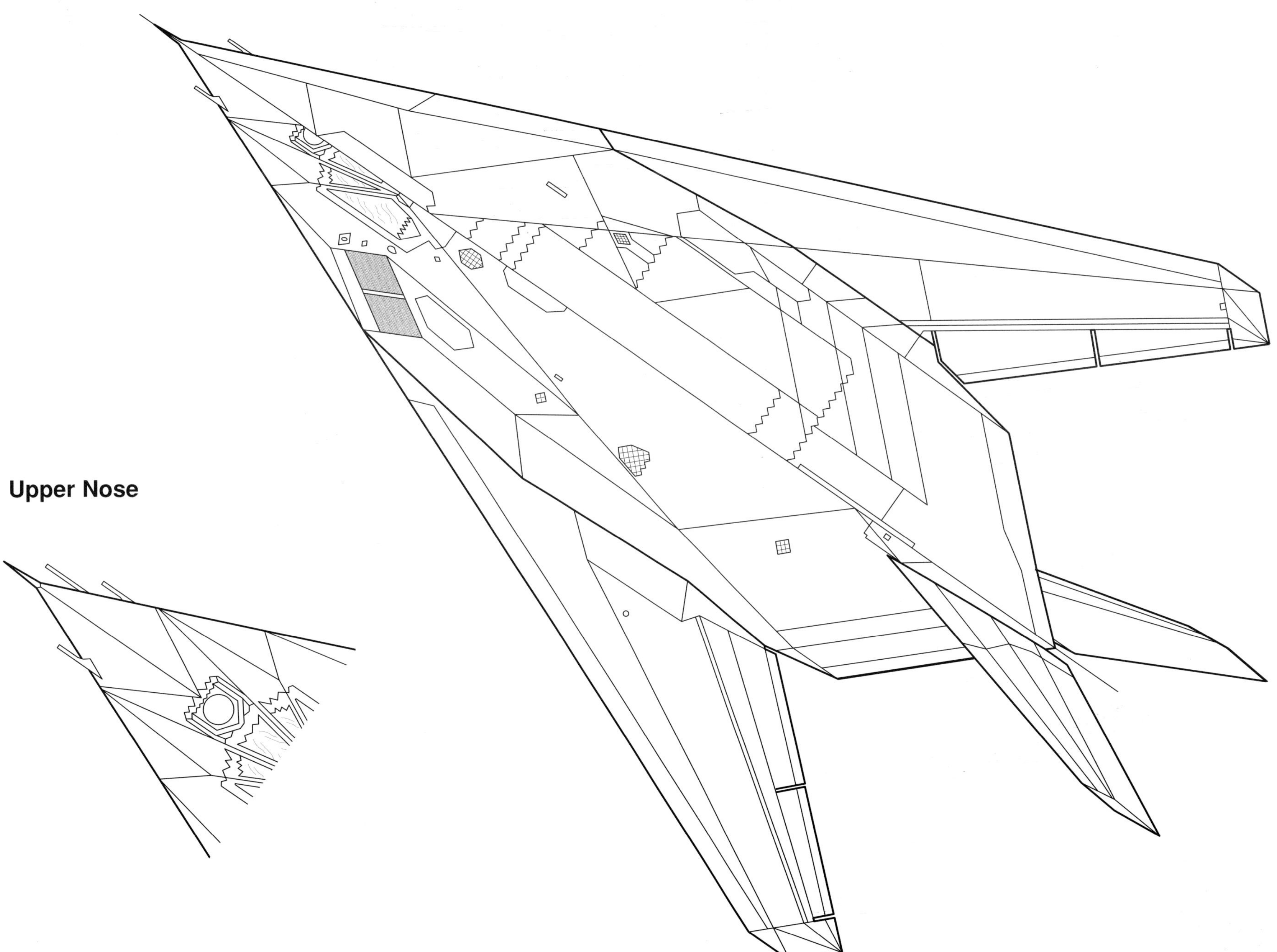
Upper Nose

Main Instrument Panel

A pilot 'flies' a night mission in a F-117A flight simulator, which included a pre-OCIP Phase 3 cockpit. These Texas Instruments Multi-function Display Indicators (MDIs) were green and white on earlier Nighthawk cockpits. They have since been replaced with full-color CMDIs. Air Force operating procedures require that the port MDI/CMDI must display primary flight data at all times. The pilot used kneeboards to keep his charts and mission data within easy reach. (Lockheed Martin)

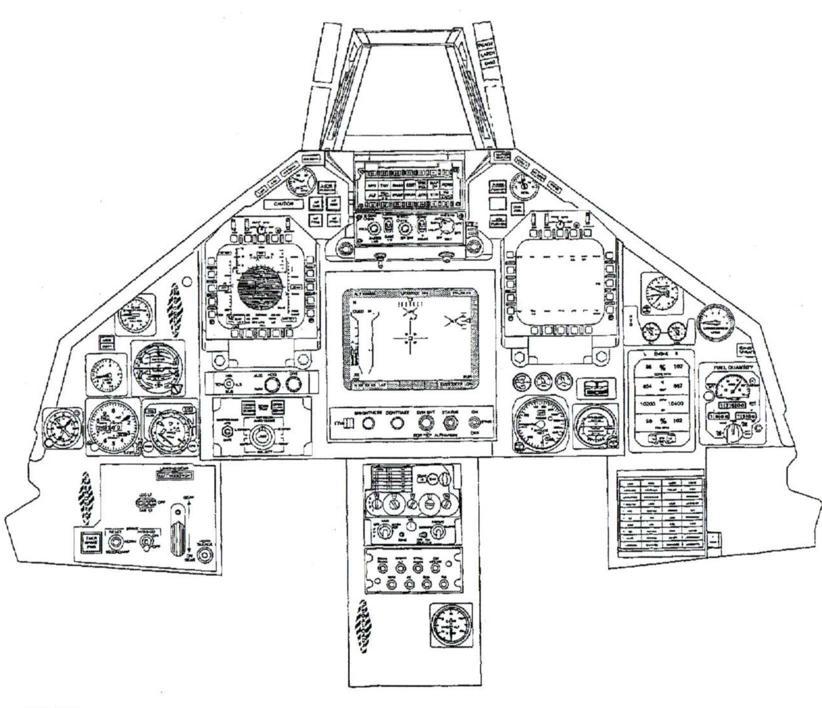

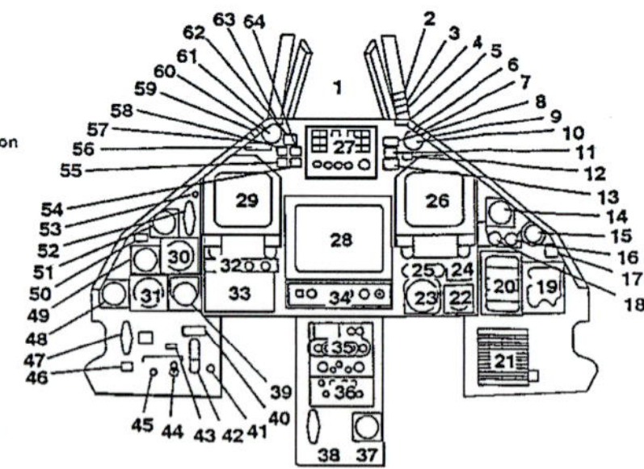

1. HUD PDU
2. Air Refueling READY Light
4. Air Refueling LATCH Light
5. MARKER BEACON Light
6. IFF MODE 4 Light
8. AR OPEN Light
9. Inlet Grid WIPER Light
10. BETA Indicator
11. Blank
12. DUAL FCS Light
13. APU Fuel Cutoff Switchlight
14. Accelerometer
15. LIQUID OXYGEN Quantity Indicator
16. UTIL Hydraulic System Pressure Indicator
17. CANOPY UNSAFE Light
18. FLT Hydraulic System Pressure Indicator
19. FUEL QUANTITY Indicator
20. ENGINE Performance Indicator
21. Annunciator Panel
22. Standby Attitude Indicator
23. RADAR Altitude Indicator
24. Turn and Slip Indicator
25. PITCH, ROLL, YAW Indicator
26. Right CMDI
27. Data Entry Panel (DEP)
28. IRADS Sensor Display
29. Left CMDI
30. Attitude Director Indicator
31. Altimeter
32. AUX NAV Panel
33. Armament Control Panel
34. IRADS Sensor Display Controls
35. UHF Radio Control Panel
36. ICS Control Panel
37. CABIN PRESS ALT Indicator
38. PEDAL ADJ Handle
39. Horizontal Situation Indicator
40. LANDING GEAR Indicator Lights
41. Landing Gear HORN SILENCE Button
42. Landing GEAR Control Handle
43. LDG/TAXI LT Switch
44. BRAKE ANTI SKID Switch
45. BRAKE System Select Switch
46. EMER BRAKE PWR Switchlight
47. EMER GEAR Extension T-Handle
48. 24 Hour Clock
49. Airspeed Indicator
50. Hook Down Switchlight
57. L BID Light
58. A/P DISC Light
59. R BID Light
60. ANGLE OF ATTACK Indicator
61. ANT DOWN Light
62. Left Engine FIRE Warning and Fuel Cutoff Switchlight
63. RLS DOWN Light
64. A/T DISC Light

The Pilot's Head-Up Display (HUD) atop the instrument panel shroud features two angled pieces of glass with a metal frame. The HUD shows the pilot basic flight data – including speed, altitude, and target sighting – without his having to look down into the cockpit. Immediately below the HUD is a Liquid Crystal Display (LCD) for showing the F-117A's attack profile and autopilot modes. Function sort keys are placed above and below the LCD. (Lockheed Martin)

Left Sidewall   Right Sidewall

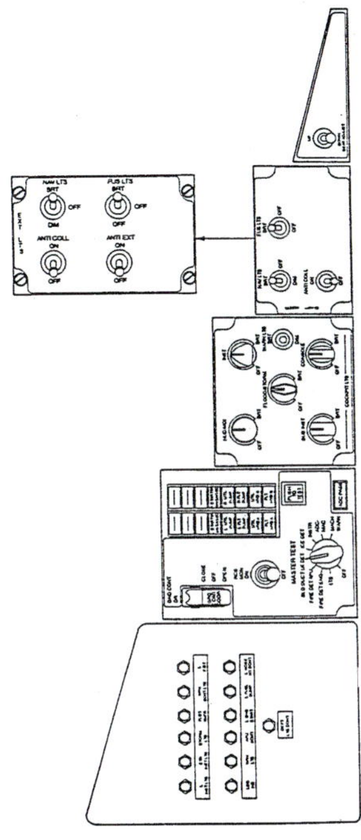

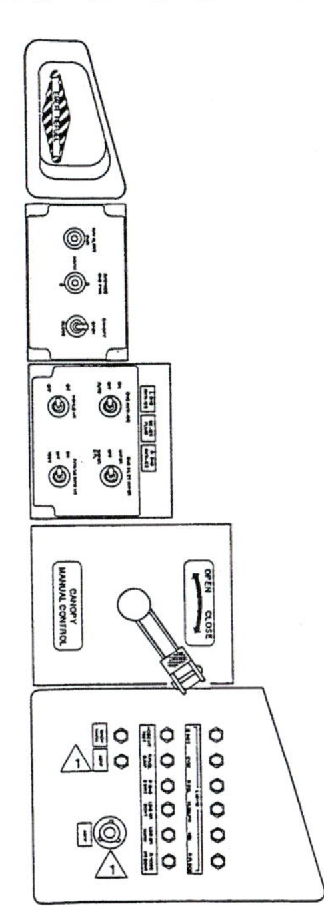

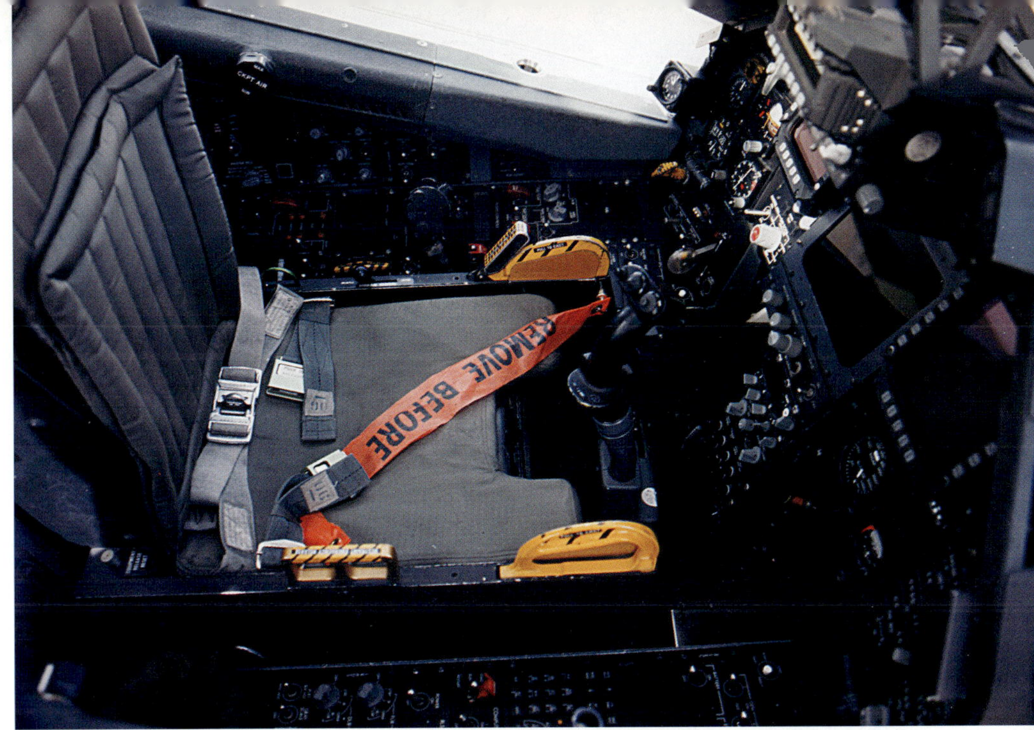

The cockpit of the F-117A is similar to that of the other newer-generation fighters in today's Air Force inventory. Most flight instruments used are 'off the shelf,' an exception being the F-117A's center screen. This screen is part of the IRAD (Infra-Red Acquisition and Designation) system for use with the infrared targeting system. (Lockheed Martin)

The master warning light panel – alerting the pilot to problems anywhere on the aircraft – is mounted immediately ahead of the starboard side console. The canopy lock handle is mounted above the upper center portion of the starboard side console. The buttons and gray knob near the yellow ejection seat handle are the F-117A's INS (Inertial Navigation System) controls. (Jim Goodall)

The throttle quadrant is mounted on the F-117A's port side console, with armament safety and aircraft power switches mounted behind it. Aircraft lighting switches are placed on the side panel along the cockpit wall. The yellow handle at the front corner of the seat is pulled for seat ejection. The F-117A's cockpit is painted Dark Gull Gray (FS36231) with Instrument Black (FS27038) panels. (Lockheed Martin)

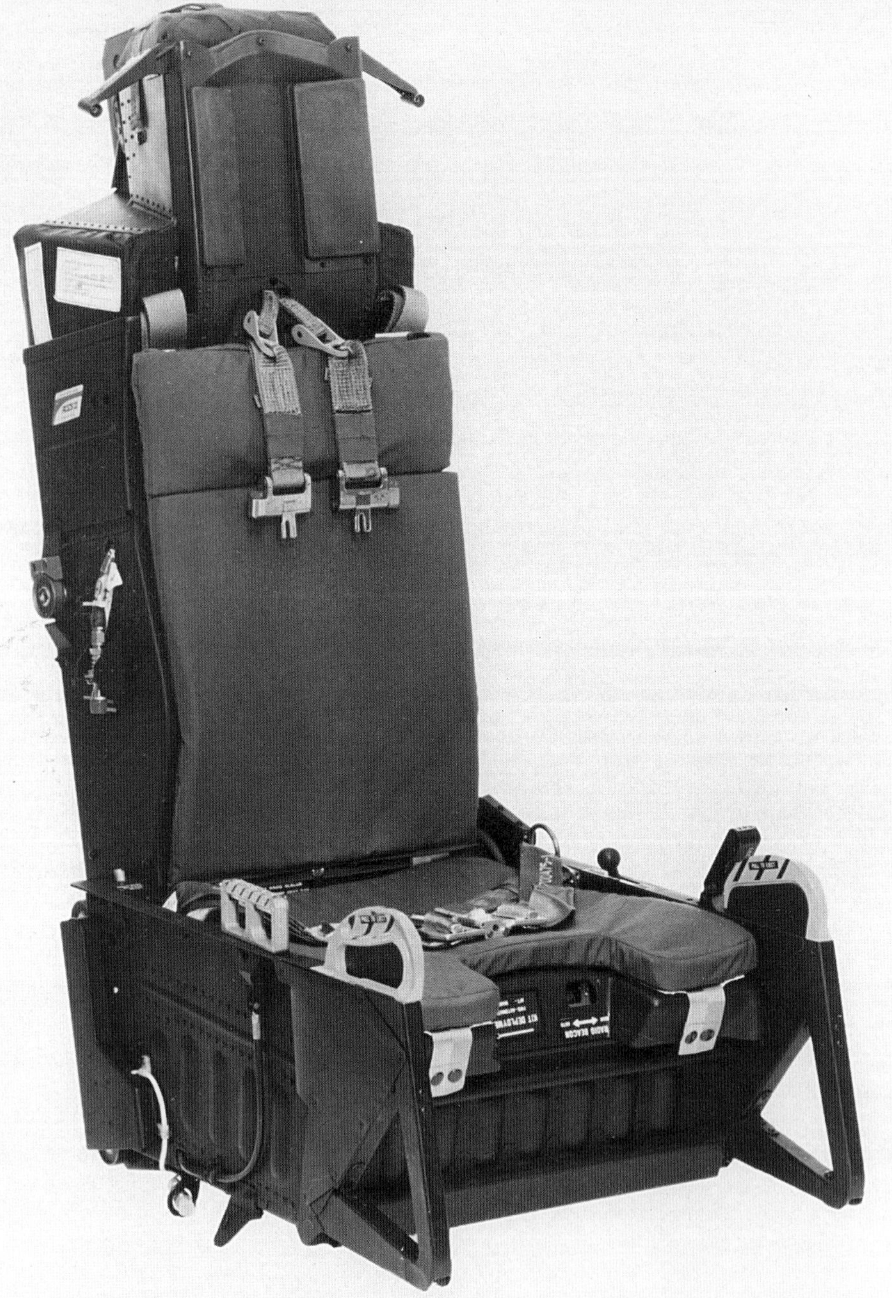

The McDonnell Douglas (now Boeing) Advanced Crew Escape System II (ACES II) ejection seat is fitted to the F-117A Nighthawk. The seat is overall Flat Black (FS37038) with cushions in a Medium Olive Drab (approximately FS34201). The two shoulder harness straps are secured to the seat just below the headrest. The seat ejection handles are yellow with black stripping. The pilot's survival kit is placed under the seat. (McDonnell Douglas)

The ACES II seat is fitted with a ballistic escape system rocket mounted in a brass colored tube on the seat's back side. The ACES II is a 'zero-zero' seat, allowing ejections from zero altitude and zero airspeed. The pilot could eject at altitudes up to 40,000 feet (12,192 M) and at airspeeds up to 600 knots (690.9 MPH, 1111.9 KMH). The rocket motor burns out approximately one half second after ejection is initiated. (McDonnell Douglas)

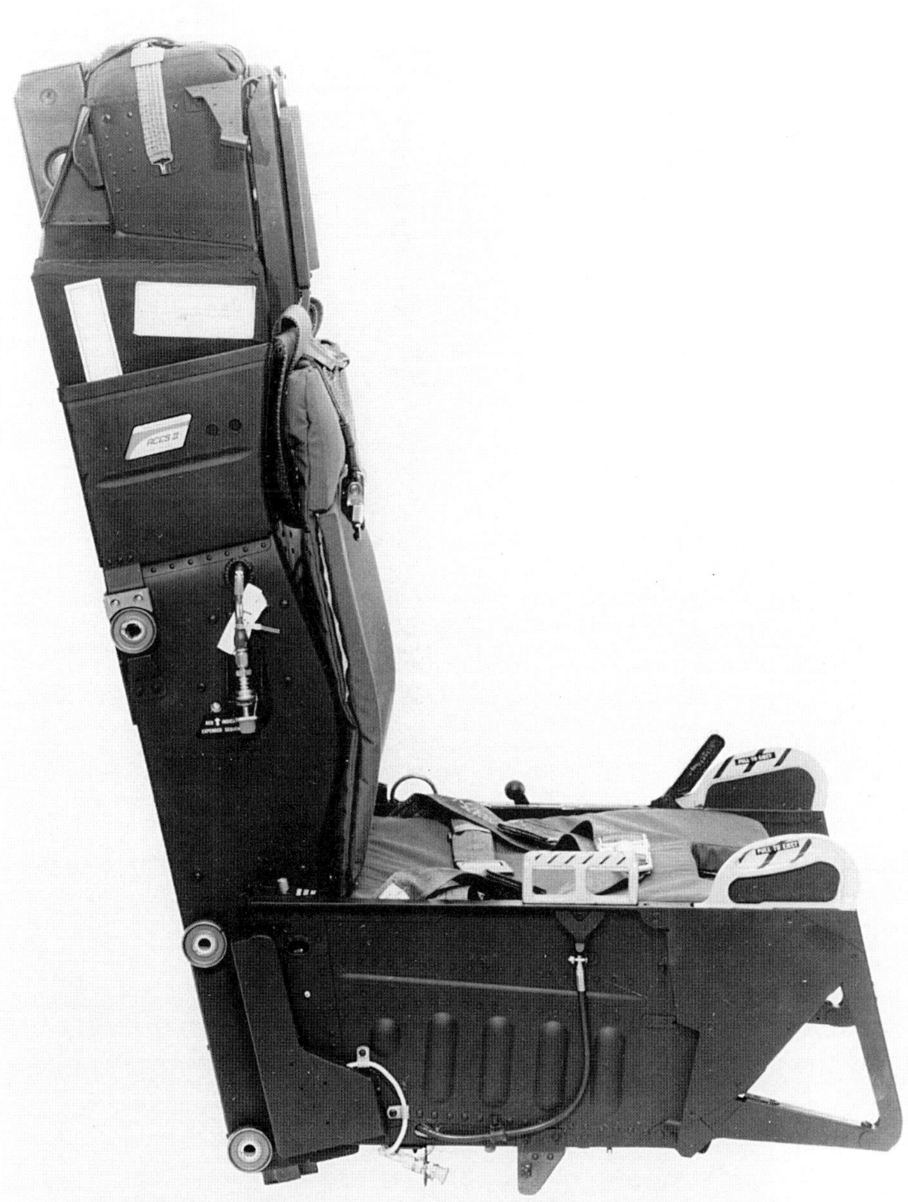

The yellow handle along the starboard edge of the ACES II seat is the restraint emergency release handle. This handle releases the pilot's seat and shoulder belts to allow an escape when the seat was not activated in an ejection. After an ejection, these restraints are automatically released to allow the pilot to return to earth using his parachute. The emergency oxygen hose is mounted midway along the seat's side. (McDonnell Douglas)

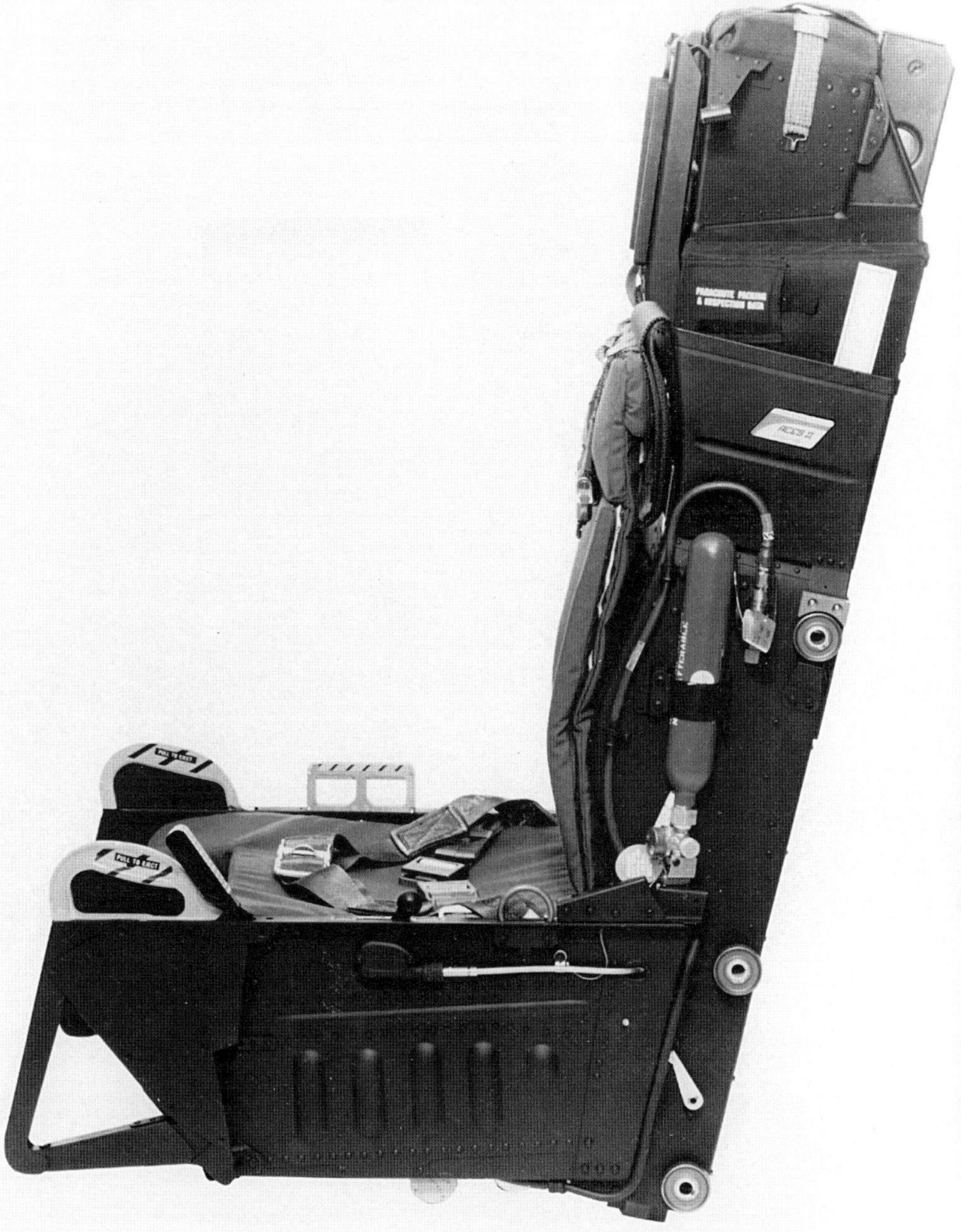

The light green bottle on the ACES II ejection seat's port side contains the emergency oxygen supply. The pilot breathes oxygen from this bottle after a high altitude ejection. The ejection controls safety lever is mounted immediately aft of the port ejection control handle. This lever prevents accidental ejection from the aircraft. The set of wheels along the seat's back fits into the aircraft's ejection seat rails. (McDonnell Douglas)

The yellow handle placed on the aft starboard instrument sidewall is the manual canopy control lever, which opens the canopy in the event of a hydraulic system failure. Circuit breakers are placed aft of the canopy handle, while a utility light is fitted near the handle's round knob end. The oxygen hose is a flexible wire-round unit covered with an Olive Drab (FS34087) Nomex sleeve. (Jim Goodall)

Red covers were placed over the fuel pump switches of the YF-117A's aft port side console. These covers prevented the pilot from accidentally hitting the toggle switches. The curled hose on the panel was connected to the pilot's G-suit, which he wore over the lower part of his body. Air from this hose filled bladders inside the G-suit during high G (gravity) maneuvers. These bladders prevented blood from pooling below the pilot's chest, which would otherwise result in a blackout. (Jim Goodall)

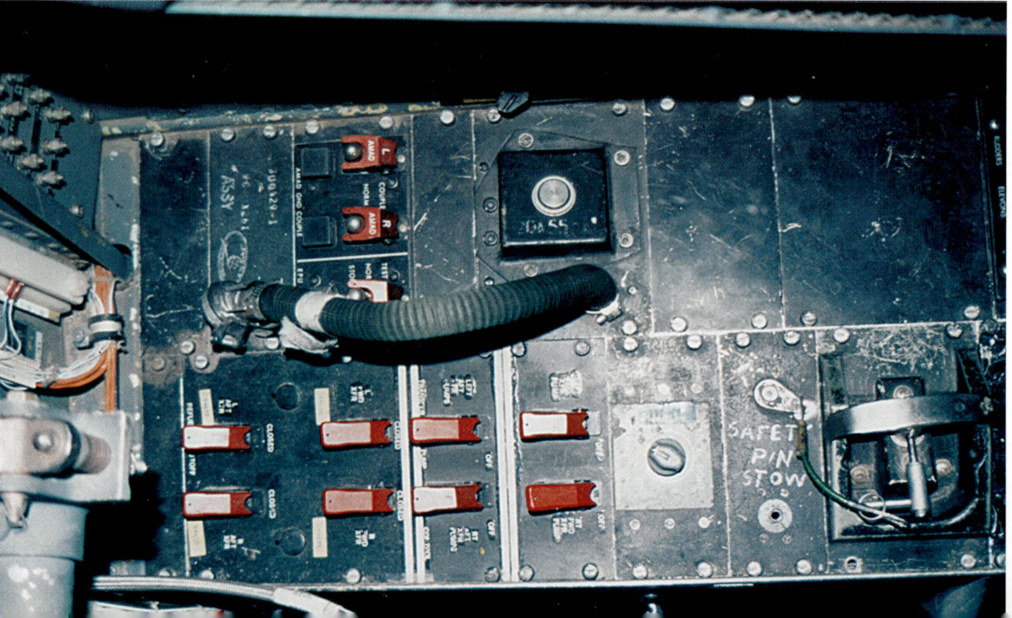

Aft of the instrument panel, the YF-117A's cockpit arrangement was virtually identical to that found on production F-117As. The pilot's oxygen hose – which connected with his face mask during flight – is draped long the starboard console. The oxygen hose was connected to a socket beside the seat. A 'Grimes light' – used for utility purposes by the pilot – is attached to a coiled handle at the aft end of the starboard console. (Jim Goodall)

The ACES II ejection seat installed in the F-117A's cockpit has silver-gray shoulder harness and lap belts with aluminum buckles. The light green bottle fitted to the seat's port side provided emergency oxygen to the pilot in the event of a high altitude ejection. The Dark Gull Gray (FS36231) control stick installed immediately forward of the seat has a black plastic grip. Dust and sun bleaching have slightly lightened the console's Instrument Black (FS27038) finish (Jim Goodall)

The back of the ACES II ejection seat rests against Dark Gull Gray (FS36231) rails placed along the aft cockpit wall. Beside the port seat rail are bundles of wiring for the cockpit's various electrical systems. The sills of the F-117A are painted Dark Gull Gray on the inner assembly and a pale gray to white color on the outboard half of the canopy sill. (Jim Goodall)

The two canopy jack screws flank the headrest of the F-117A's ACES II ejection seat. These anodized gold jack screws raise and lower the canopy using hydraulic power. The two pitot sensor inlets projecting from the ejection seat's top collect air data used to determine the automatic separation of the pilot from his seat after ejection. The cockpit is pressurized with air bled from the two engines, which is either heated or cooled before being sent to the cockpit. (Jim Goodall)

29

The F-117A is fitted with unique grilled engine inlets just above the wing root. This grill absorbs radar returns, which would normally reflect on the engine compressor inside the inlet. The spring-loaded intake suction relief door above helps offset the inlet's poor performance. This door usually opens on engine start and take-off, when the engine requires more air. (Tony Landis)

The inlet wiper blade is deployed in the mid-sweep position; normally, this blade is normally in the stowed position in the box just below and forward of the inlet lip. There was a proposal to possibly retrofit the F-117A's inlets to more closely resemble those of the B-2A stealth bomber. This would have deleted the time and labor intensive inlet screens and given the engine inlet a serpentine pattern, with the engine face away from direct view from the front. This plan was cancelled due to the F-117A's age. (Paul Crickmore)

The intake suction relief door fits flush over the inlet. Immediately below the inlet is the de-icing air duct, which blows heated air across the intake grill to melt ice forming on the grill. This ice would greatly reduce airflow into the engine. The vertically mounted wiper blade recessed in front of and below the inlet cleans off the ice build up. (Jim Goodall)

The inlet de-icing wiper is a pale gray color, in contrast to the overall black finish of the F-117A. The engine inlet is set back aft of the wing's leading edge to reduce radar returns from below the aircraft. The bumps and waves found on the Nighthawk's surface result from the Radar Absorbent Material (RAM), which was applied in layers over the entire surface. (Jim Goodall)

The F-117A's mid-fuselage consists of a series of faceted surfaces, which extend aft from the upper canopy area. Immediately aft of the national insignia is one of two radar reflectors mounted on the Nighthawk for training and non-tactical ferry missions. These reflectors – removable for combat and operational training missions – produce a return on air traffic control radars. The F-117A's radar signature – approximately the size of a small bird – would prevent its easy detection by radar without these reflectors. (Jim Goodall)

The refueling boom from a McDonnell Douglas KC-10A Extender is connected with an F-117A's refueling receptacle. The receptacle rotates 180˚ when not in use. The two panels immediately ahead of the refueling receptacle house ILS (Instrument Landing System) glideslope antennas. (USAF via G. Phillips)

A red anti-collision light is mounted on the F-117A's port upper fuselage to warn nearby aircraft under peacetime conditions. Aft and to port of this light is the left engine bleed-air heat exchanger exhaust. Excess heat from bleed air cooled for environmental systems is removed through this port. The 'Cadillac fins' on the forward outboard lips of the exhaust ejectors improve air flow around this area. (Jim Goodall)

A 37th TFW F-117A on display at a base open house shows the Nighthawk's faceted surface, which deflects radar waves from the aircraft. The landing gear doors were designed to protect the gear bays from radar reflections, which would otherwise highlight the F-117A's presence. The names of the pilot on the canopy rail and the maintenance crew on the nose gear door are white. (USAF via G. Phillips)

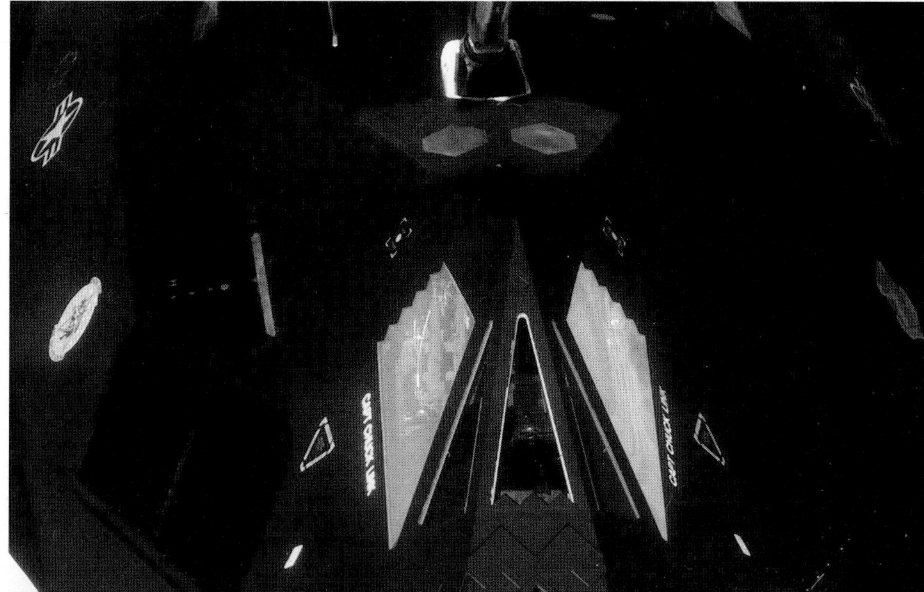

An F-117A assigned to the commander of the 49th Fighter Wing (FW) prepares to depart its hangar at Holloman Air Force Base (AFB), New Mexico on a night training mission. An SUU-20 practice bomb and rocket dispenser is loaded on each of the two weapons bay trapezes. This dispenser held six 3 lb (1.4 kg) BDU-33 practice bombs; the four rocket launch tubes are not used by F-117As. The Nighthawk's elevons drooped when hydraulic pressure bled off from these surfaces. The firewall separating the twin hangar bays can withstand a 1000° F (537.8° C) fire for 90 minutes before the fire burns through the firewall. Each hangar at Holloman houses two F-117As in temperature-controlled conditions to prevent degradation of the aircraft's radar absorbent materials by the desert climate. (Tony Landis)

The fourth FSD (Full Scale Development) YF-117A (79-10784) releases a 2000 lb (907.2 KG) GBU-27 laser guided bomb (LGB) during weapons testing. Two faded red pods under the aircraft's wings housed cameras used to film the bomb's release for evaluation purposes. The GBU-27's center body was painted red for this test, while the seeker and tail assembly remained Olive Drab (FS34087). Black striping on the weapons bay door allowed the camera to capture the relationship between the bomb's angle of release and the aircraft's body. (Lockheed Martin)

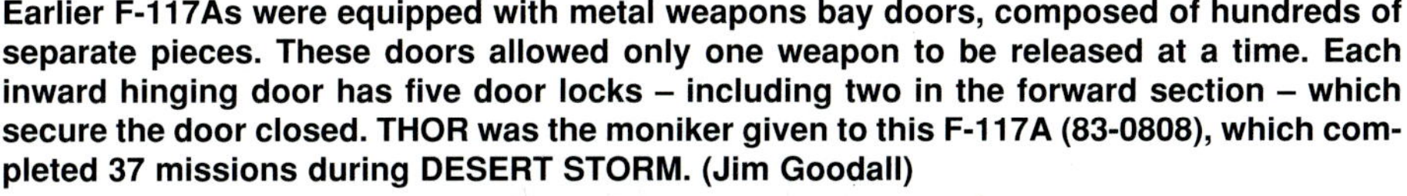

F-117As were retrofitted with composite weapons bay doors between 1987 and 1992. These new doors are lighter and easier to maintain than the previous metal covers. The composite doors also permit both weapons bay doors to open simultaneously without fear of flutter or deflection of the door due to extreme turbulence. This F-117A (84-0825) was nicknamed MAD-MAX and flew 33 missions in Operation DESERT STORM. (Jim Goodall)

Earlier F-117As were equipped with metal weapons bay doors, composed of hundreds of separate pieces. These doors allowed only one weapon to be released at a time. Each inward hinging door has five door locks – including two in the forward section – which secure the door closed. THOR was the moniker given to this F-117A (83-0808), which completed 37 missions during DESERT STORM. (Jim Goodall)

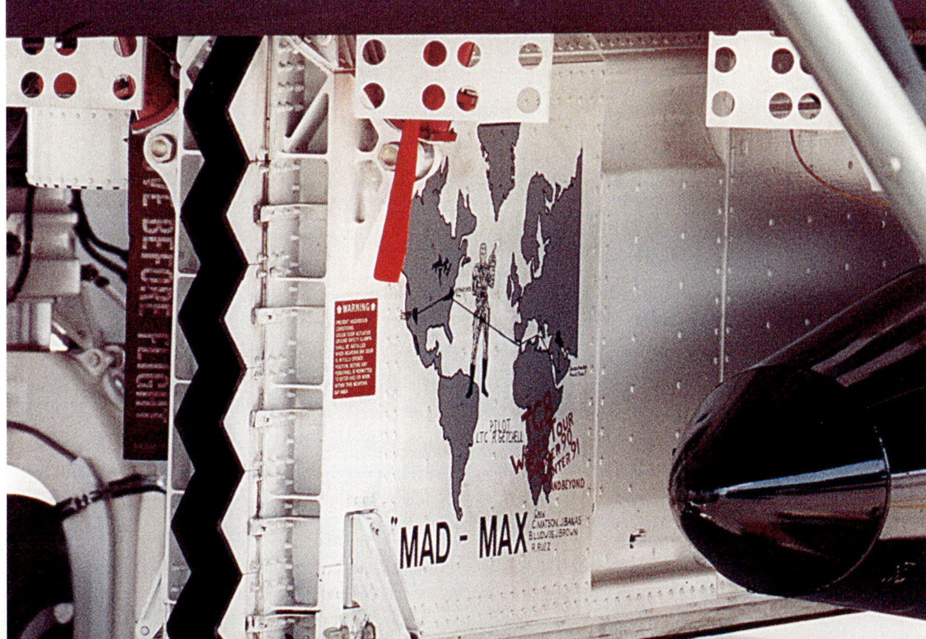

Air Force ground crewmen transport a practice 2000 pound (907.2 KG) GBU-27 Laser Guided Bomb (LGB) to a 49th Fighter Wing (FW) F-117A (84-0828) at Holloman AFB, New Mexico. The blue band around the weapon's forward section indicates an inert bomb. The seeker head – also called a computer controlled guidance (CCG) unit – and the forward fins will be attached to the GBU-27 when the bomb is loaded into the Nighthawk's weapons bay. Red REMOVE BEFORE FLIGHT tags were fitted to the GBU-27's aft tail fin and fuse wires. These tags remind the ground crewmen to arm the weapons before the aircraft takes off. (Lockheed Martin)

Ground crewmen use an MJ-1 lift truck to bring an inert 2000 pound GBU-27 LGB towards the port weapons bay of a 37th Tactical Fighter Wing (TFW) F-117A. The F-117A can carry a 2000-pound bomb in each bay. The MJ-1 is a standard Air Force mechanized hoist vehicle used to load munitions onto aircraft. The GBU-27's laser seeker head is placed in a storage box near the Nighthawk's nose landing gear. This seeker head would be installed on the bomb once the weapon was loaded onto the F-117A's weapons bay trapeze. The four nose fins – packed into the box next to the one holding the seeker head – would then be fitted to the seeker head. (Lockheed Martin)

An Air Force ground crewman arms a practice GBU-27 LGB loaded onto an F-117A's port weapons bay trapeze. Removing the safety pins with their REMOVE BEFORE FLIGHT tags arms the weapon. US bombs are painted overall Olive Drab (FS34087); the seeker head and the band around the bomb's front are Dark Blue (FS35109) to indicate a training weapon. The two white perforated plates deployed ahead of each weapons bay are air deflectors. These air deflectors extend when the bay doors are opened to improve airflow for bomb release. The deflectors retract when the weapons bay doors are closed. (Lockheed Martin)

2000 lb (907.2 KG) GBU-10 Paveway II Laser-Guided Bomb (LGB)

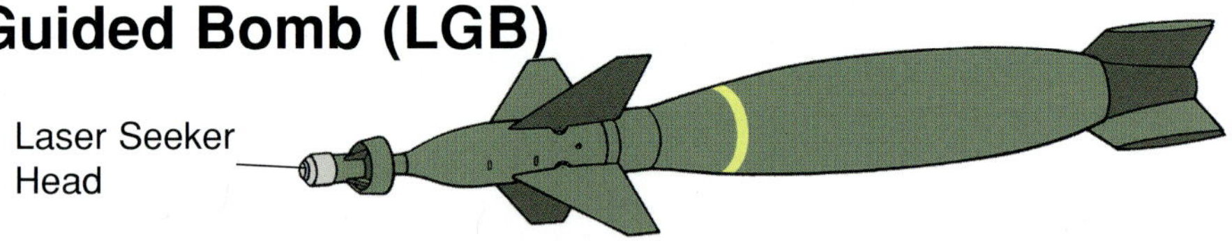

Laser Seeker
Head

2000 lb GBU-27 LGB

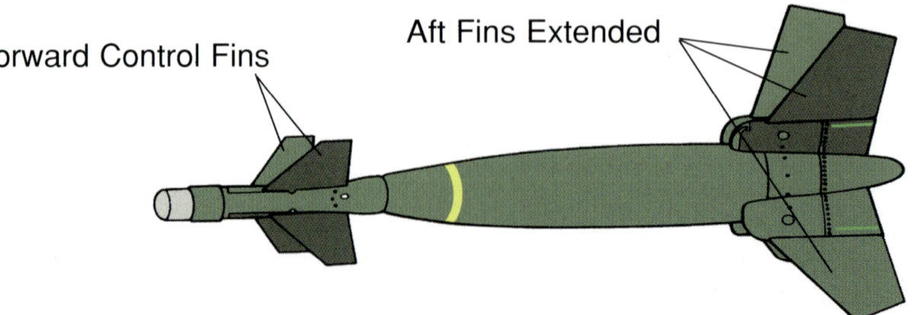

A weapons technician prepares to install the laser seeker head to a 2000 pound GBU-10 Paveway II laser guided bomb, which was fitted to the F-117A's port weapons bay trapeze. The weapon and the seeker are always shipped in separate containers to prevent the possibility of the weapon detonating accidentally. The seeker head focuses on a target 'illuminated' by a laser designator in either the launching F-117A, another aircraft, or from a Forward Air Controller (FAC) on the ground. (Paul Crickmore collection)

The F-117A's port weapons bay trapeze was swung down and forward for weapon loading. Trapeze and door movements are synchronized to allow minimal disruption of the aircraft's low observable status during weapons delivery. The interior of the weapons bay and the trapeze are Gloss White (FS17875). Black stripes were applied to this weapons bay door interior for weapons testing; operational Nighthawks do not have this striping. (Tom Tulus)

2000 lb GBU-24 Paveway III LGB

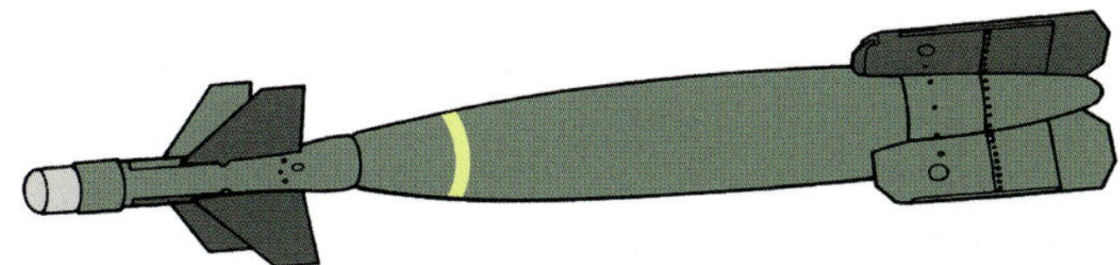

Insignia of the Dragon Test Team, nickname for Detachment 1, 49th Fighter Weapons Wing at Nellis Air Force Base, Nevada. Det 1 personnel performed Follow-On Testing and Evaluation (FOT&E) on the F-117A.

The F-117A weapons bay area measures 15 feet 5 inches (4.7 M) long by 5 feet 9 inches (1.8 M) wide. Each bay can accommodate a 2000 pound (907.2 KG) bomb or an Air-to-Surface Missile (ASM). Bundles of electrical wiring run along the inboard side of the Nighthawk's starboard weapons bay, whose trapeze was removed. Lockheed designed a camera/sensor pallet for the RF-117A reconnaissance version; however, this variant was cancelled by the Air Force. (Tom Tulus)

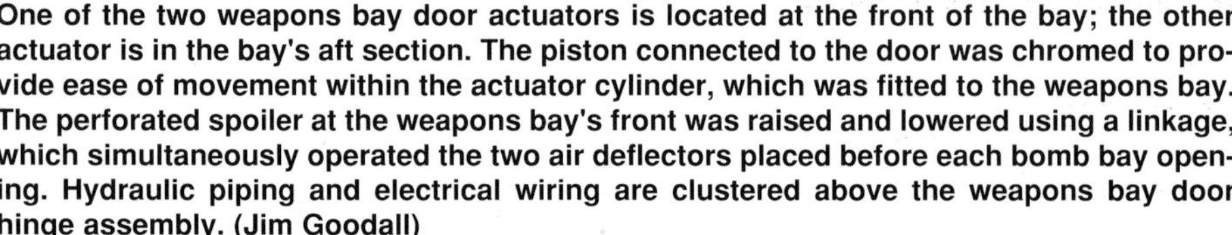

One of the two weapons bay door actuators is located at the front of the bay; the other actuator is in the bay's aft section. The piston connected to the door was chromed to provide ease of movement within the actuator cylinder, which was fitted to the weapons bay. The perforated spoiler at the weapons bay's front was raised and lowered using a linkage, which simultaneously operated the two air deflectors placed before each bomb bay opening. Hydraulic piping and electrical wiring are clustered above the weapons bay door hinge assembly. (Jim Goodall)

The robust weapons bay door actuator attachment is mounted on the inboard side of the F-117A's weapons bay. Door lock attachment points are fitted to the outboard sides of the door and fit into door locks on the weapons bay side when closed. A 2000 pound GBU-27 Laser Guided Bomb (LGB) is mounted on the Nighthawk's trapeze. This trapeze and the bay door operate quickly to avoid compromising the aircraft's stealth characteristics. Black stripes placed on the weapons bay door's inner surface were for weapons test calibration and are not seen on operational aircraft. (Jim Goodall)

The F-117A's weapons bay trapeze is hinged on two A-shaped frames mounted to the forward and aft ends of the trapeze. Sway braces connecting the bomb with the trapeze prevent the weapon from shifting sideways during flight. The Orange Yellow (FS33538) stripe on the bomb's body indicates this is an actual weapon. The two weapons bay deflectors were lowered at the front when the bay door was opened. (Jim Goodall)

The F-117A's weapons bay trapeze is hydraulically operated in coordination with the opening or closing of the weapons bay. When the Nighthawk's IRAD (Infra-Red Acquisition and Detection) system acquires the target, the weapons bay opens and the trapeze is lowered. The weapon is quickly released from the trapeze, which is then retracted and the door closed. (Jim Goodall)

The fore-and-aft weapons bay trapeze provides a strong, yet lightweight frame to support the lowered trapeze and the weapon mounted on it. This trapeze assembly allows bombs of up to 2000 pounds (907.2 KG) in weight or air-to-surface missiles to be completely enclosed within the weapons bay until the moment of release from the aircraft. (Jim Goodall)

Each weapon carried by the F-117A's trapeze – including this 2000 lb LGB – is secured to the trapeze through two lugs on the bomb's upper body. These two lugs are spaced 30 inches (76.2 CM) apart and fit into a bomb rack attached to the trapeze. This rack is fitted with four sway braces – two per side – to prevent the weapon from rocking sideways prior to release. (Jim Goodall)

This insignia was used by Lockheed Field Service personnel assigned to the 37th Tactical Fighter Wing (TFW) – the first operational F-117A unit – at Tonopah Test Range, Nevada. The field service representatives provided technical support to the 37th TFW and serviced as a liaison with Lockheed's engineering staff in Burbank, California. This patch incorporates the F-117A, the Nighthawk, and the Skunk Works' skunk.

Members of the 410th Flight Test Squadron load a Lockheed Martin AGM-158 JASSM (Joint Standoff Air-to-Surface Missile) into a YF-117A (79-10782) at Air Force Plant 42, Site 7 in Palmdale, California. The JASSM is loaded into the weapons bay using a standard Air Force MJ-1 weapons loader. This weapon is a low-observable cruise missile with a 1000 pound (453.6 KG) warhead and a range of 115 miles (185.1 KM). (Lockheed Martin)

Lockheed Martin AGM-158 JASSM (Joint Standoff Air-to-Surface Missile)

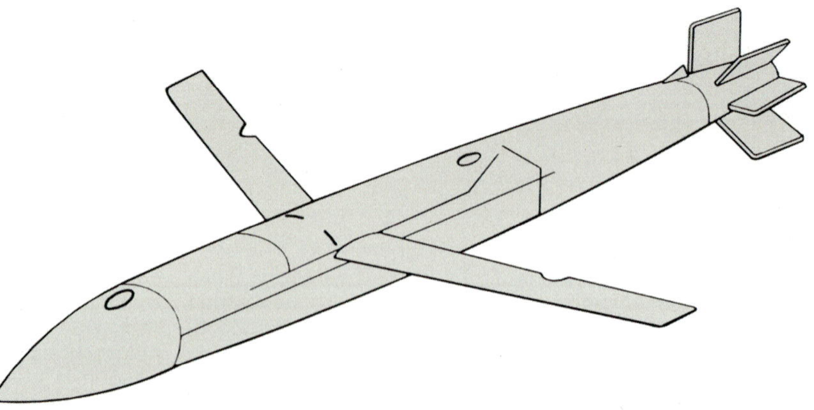

The F-117A is cleared to carry a variety of weapons, including the B61 and B57 tactical thermonuclear bombs displayed in front of the aircraft. These nuclear weapons were used prior to the advent of 'smart weapons.' Arrayed to the aircraft's right (back to front) are: 2000 lb (907.2 KG) GBU-10 Paveway II Laser Guided Bomb (LGB); 500 lb (226.8 KG) GBU-12 LGB; SUU-30 Cluster Bomb Unit (CBU); 500 lb conventional bomb; and SUU-21 practice bomb dispenser. Displayed to the F-117A's left are: GBU-10 LGB; 2000 lb conventional bomb; SUU-64 CBU; and CBU-55 Fuel Air Explosive (FAE) bomb. Not displayed are the 'smart weapons': the AGM-158 Joint Standoff Air-to-Surface Missile (JASSM); the Boeing Joint Direct Attack Munitions (JDAM); and the Raytheon AGM-154 Joint Stand-Off Weapon (JSOW). (Lockheed Martin)

This insignia was assigned to the 410th Flight Test Squadron (FTS), 412th Test Wing. This unit was the US Air Force's F-117A flight test organization at Palmdale, California and was established in 1984.

Boeing JDAM (Joint Direct Attack Munitions)

Raytheon AGM-154 JSOW (Joint Stand-Off Weapon)

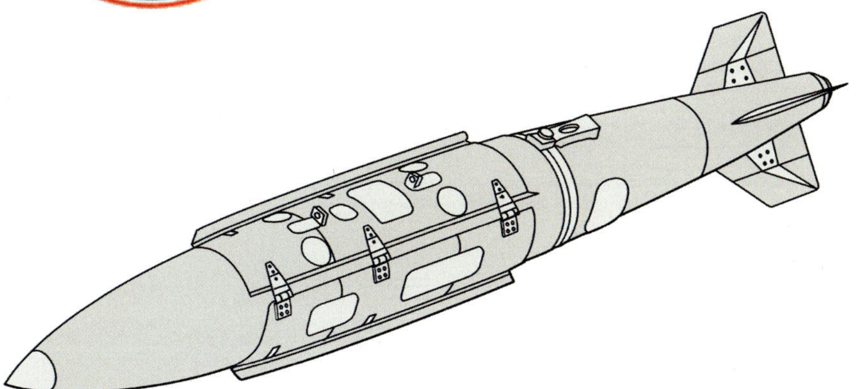

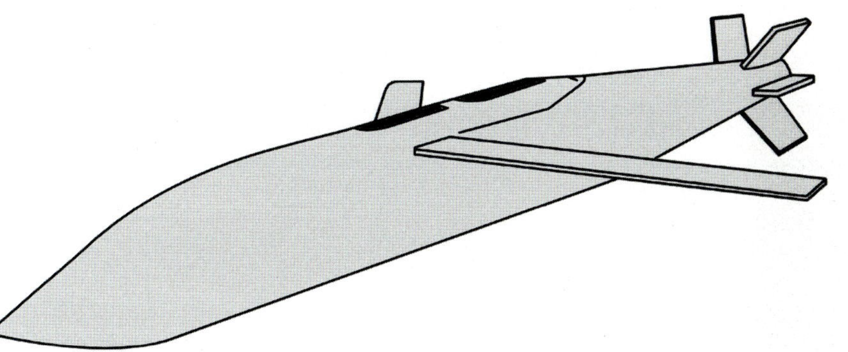

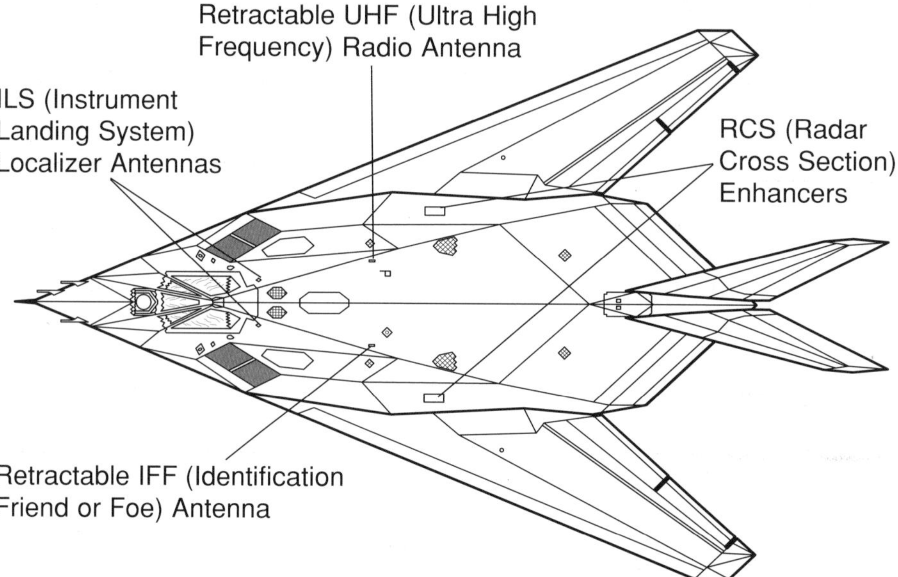

Upper Surface Antenna Locations

An 37th TFW F-117A (86-0839) is parked beside a taxiway at King Khalid Air Base, Saudi Arabia during Operation DESERT SHIELD in 1990. The Nighthawk's upper fuselage slopes downward from the top of the canopy to the tail section. The area immediately aft of the national insignia on the fuselage held the radar reflector used during peacetime training flights. (USAF via G. Phillips)

An F-117A (82-0804) on final approach flies over the fence line eight miles (12.9 KM) north of Tonopah Test Range, Nevada in mid-1990. A red flush-mounted anti-collision light is fitted starboard of the nose landing gear strut. The red L-shaped marking on the aft fuselage was placed over the emergency arrestor hook cover. This cover would be jettisoned and the hook deployed to engage arrestor cables at an airfield in the event of a brake failure. (Tony Landis)

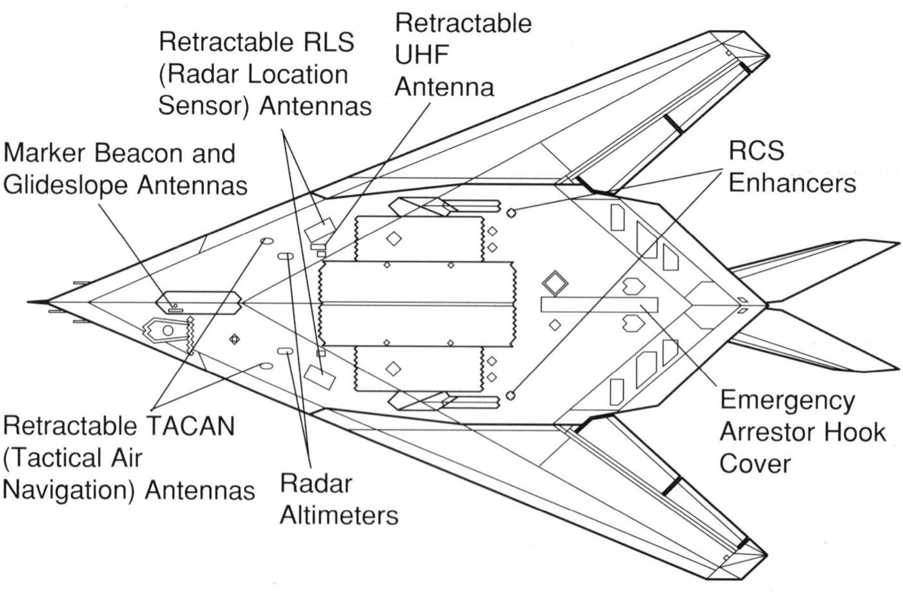

Lower Surface Antenna Locations

The F-117A is fitted with radar reflectors on the mid-fuselage sides for training and non-combat flights. These reflectors have metal shapes inside that create a large radar return, allowing air traffic control to detect the Nighthawk and monitor our crowded skies. Flush screws fasten the radar reflector to the aircraft when in use. The national insignia is painted Light Gray (approximately FS36495). (Jim Goodall)

F-117A with Landing Gear Extended

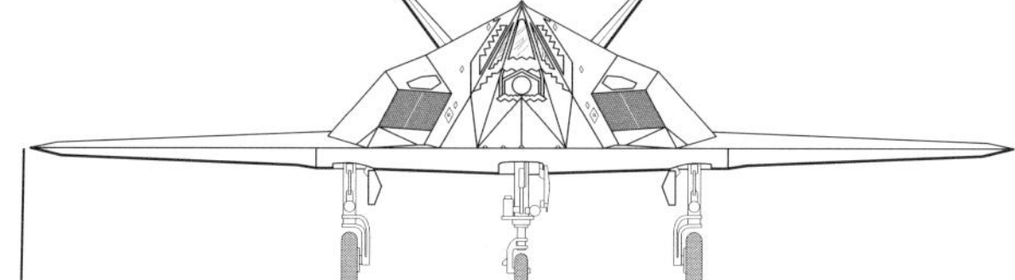

Height from Ground to Wingtip is 5 ft 11 in (1.8 м)

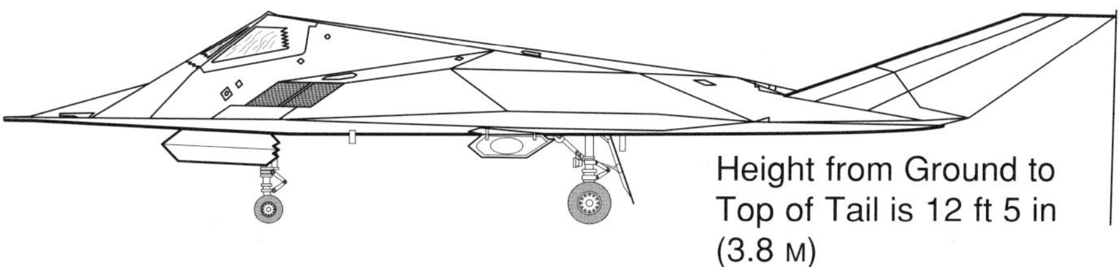

Height from Ground to Top of Tail is 12 ft 5 in (3.8 м)

Two doors cover each F-117A main landing gear: one door immediately aft of the gear strut and the other door farther ahead. The round tube just behind the main gear was an early radar reflector, which used a jack-point attachment to the aircraft. This reflector proved to be too much of a maintenance headache for continued use as it would vibrate in the air stream and could sometimes break off or come unscrewed. (Tony Landis)

The F-117A's Menasco landing gear features one nose wheel and two main wheels. Each landing gear strut is fitted with a landing light, which is turned on during approach, landing, and ground taxiing at night. These white lights provide forward illumination for the pilot and easier visual tracking from the ground. Chocks placed on the main wheels prevent the Nighthawk from rolling on the ground if the brakes were released. (Tony Landis)

(Above) The F-117A's main landing gear retracts forward into the gear bay and is covered by two gear doors. The aft-hinged strut door is attached to the main gear strut above the scissor link. The forward door encloses the tire and wheel assembly. The port weapons bay door was opened on this displayed F-117A to reveal an MXU-648 travel pod mounted on the trapeze. This pod – an empty BLU-1/27 fire bomb case – is used to carry the pilot's personal effects on deployments away from the home base. The MXU-648's side hatch was opened for access to the pod's storage space. This pod was painted black and decorated with the insignia of the Tactical Air Command (TAC) to port of the opening and the 37th TFW to starboard. (Jim Goodall)

(Left) The YF-117A's basic main landing gear configuration was retained in production Nighthawks; however, the F-117A's gear assembly has approximately twice the mass found on the SENIOR TREND prototypes. Landing gear assemblies, bays, and door interiors are Gloss White (FS17875), while the oleo (shock absorbing) strut is left in natural chromed metal for smooth operation. Hydraulic hoses run down the aft side of the gear strut – including the scissor link connecting the upper and lower strut sections – to the wheel brakes. This YF-117A and other Nighthawks were originally equipped with Loral steel brakes, which were later replaced with the company's lighter and stronger carbon-carbon brakes. The newer brake system improves the aircraft's crosswind stopping capability over the steel brakes. (Jim Goodall)

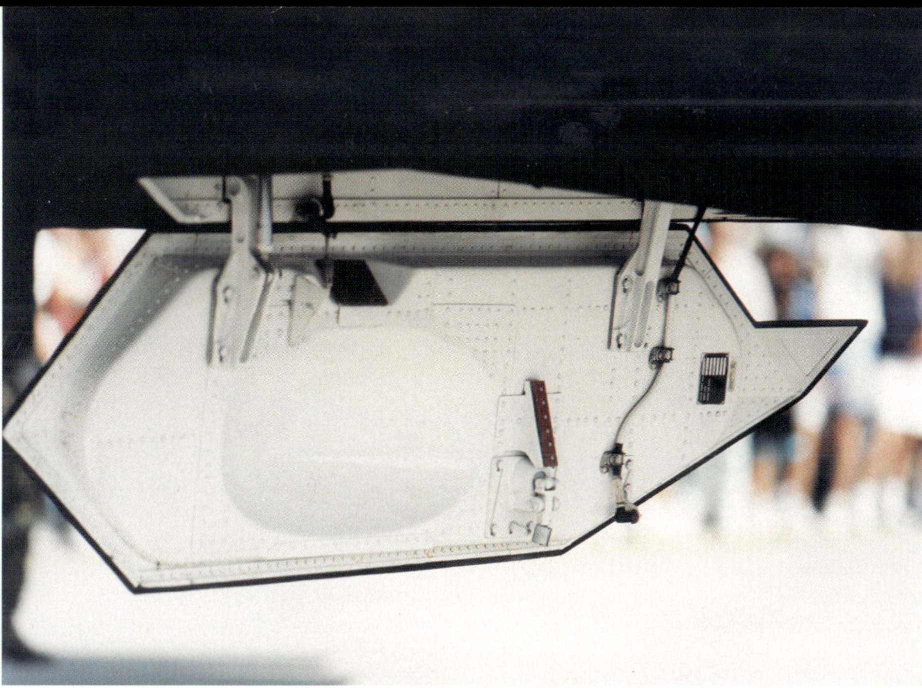

(Above) The F-117A's forward main landing gear door is hinged on the inboard side of the gear bay. This door and all other openings on the Nighthawk are faceted with specific angles and shapes to deflect radar waves. A gear door lock indicator switch wire and actuator runs down the aft section of the door. The F-117A's landing gear doors use hydraulic power to retract, which insures a tight – thus, stealthy – fit. A bulge in the door's inner surface accommodates the main gear tire when retracted. Immediately aft of this bulge is the door locking mechanism, which secures the gear door in place when the landing gear is retracted. (Jim Goodall)

(Right) The F-117A's main landing gear is fitted with Goodyear 26-ply tubeless tires, which measure 32 inches (81.3 cm) in diameter by 8.8 inches (22.4 cm) wide. The Nighthawk's early steel brake assemblies were replaced with Loral carbon-carbon brakes within F-15E Eagle wheels. These newer brakes offer greatly improved stopping power over steel brake systems. The Nighthawk's anti-skid brakes allow for braking control on wet and icy runways. The wheels have 12 openings on the outboard side to allow air to cool the brake assembly. A yellow air stem for the tire is located within the rearmost wheel opening. All landing gear assemblies on both the YF-117A SENIOR TREND prototypes and the operational F-117As were painted Gloss White (FS17875). The landing light is mounted on the front of the main strut, immediately under the retraction strut. (Lockheed Martin)

The production F-117A's main landing gear carry-through assembly is larger and shaped differently than on the YF-117As. The wheel axle from the main strut goes through the inboard wheel surface. Each main landing gear assembly is fitted with a landing light attached just above the oleo (shock absorbing) collar. The retraction strut pulled the main gear strut up and forward into the landing gear bay. A thin strut connected the gear door with the gear strut, while two hinges secured the door to the fuselage. (Jim Goodall)

Early F-117As were equipped with Loral steel brakes and the wheels featured smaller openings than those associated with the F-15-type wheel and brake system retrofitted to the Nighthawks. A manufacturer's label placed around the upper strut assembly included maintenance instructions for ground crewmen servicing the landing gear assembly. The metal manufacturer's plate on the inside of the upper gear door area included the contract number, part number, and description. (Jim Goodall)

The F-117A's main landing gear is mounted within the mid-fuselage area, near the wing roots. The uneven appearance of the upper fuselage panels is due to the Radar Absorbent Material (RAM) applied to the Nighthawk's exterior surface. The RAM was originally applied in layers over the aluminum aircraft structure. This material was later replaced with a spray-on version, which produced a smoother shape when applied to the F-117A. (Jim Goodall)

A 37th TFW F-117A is displayed at a US Air Force Base open house. Spectators are kept well away from Nighthawks on display to prevent their damaging the sensitive RAM on the aircraft's exterior surfaces. A radar reflector for non-combat flying was installed on the port fuselage aft of the national insignia; an identical unit was carried on the starboard side. This F-117A is fitted with the early model wheels and steel brakes. (USAF via G. Phillips)

The F-117A's wide landing gear track allows for ease of handling on the ground and during cross-wind takeoffs and landings. The angles of the landing gear doors deflect radar waves from these areas of the Nighthawk, which reduces the radar signature of the aircraft. Another 'stealth' item is the upturned aft fuselage surface leading into the 'platypus' engine exhausts. These exhausts reduced the F-117A's heat signature from enemy sensors. (USAF via G. Phillips)

A 37th TFW F-117A arrives at Langley AFB, Virginia on 19 August 1990. The Nighthawk's landing gear lights are turned on for the approach and landing. The landing gear extends down and back, using the force of gravity. This feature allows for gear extension in the event the F-117A's hydraulic system fails. This Nighthawk flew into Langley from Tonopah Test Range, Nevada for an overnight stop on the way to Saudi Arabia during Operation DESERT SHIELD. (USAF via G. Phillips)

An F-117A (85-0832) assigned to the 37th TFW is parked at Tonopah Test Range, Nevada in early 1988. The Downward Looking Infra-Red (DLIR) is placed beside the nose landing gear bay, while a red anti-collision light for non-combat flights is placed aft of the DLIR. Some of the aircraft's radar absorbing black paint was worn off from the aft undersurface.

This aircraft was nicknamed ONCE BITTEN and flew 30 combat missions against Iraq in 1991. The F-117A parked in the background was 85-0835. This aircraft was dubbed THE DRAGON and flew 26 combat missions during DESERT STORM. These nicknames and related artwork were displayed inside the weapons bay doors. (Lockheed Martin)

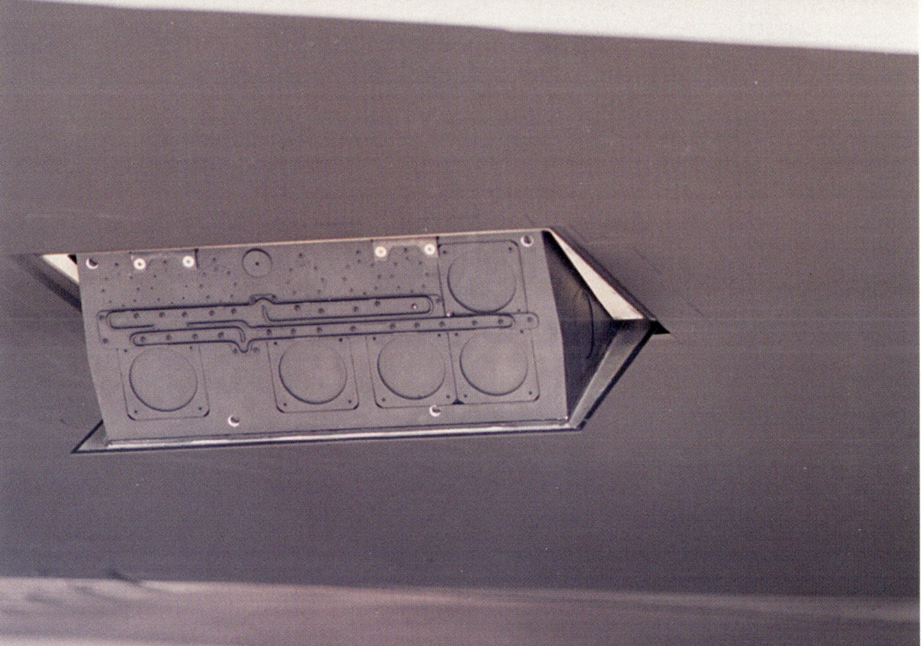

On early F-117As, two Radar Location Sensors (RLS) were located just aft of each wing's leading edge, approximately ten feet (3 м) from the aircraft's centerline. They were deployed downward only during certain phases of bombing runs. The RLS function is no longer used. (Jim Goodall)

Just beyond the port aft trailing edge of the F-117A's wing lies the port 'platypus' exhaust duct. The louver-type exhaust duct dissipates the heat generated by the engines' exhaust, reducing the Nighthawk's Infra-Red (IR) signature. Just to the outside of the exhaust ejector is a small fin – nicknamed the 'Cadillac' fin by maintenance technicians – which improves airflow in the aft fuselage area. (Jim Goodall)

The F-117A's wing is a modified delta planform, swept back 67.5˚ along its leading edge. The uneven surface of the wing was due to the layered Radar Absorbent Material (RAM) coatings. The challenge in Low Observable (LO) aircraft design is not necessarily just in the coatings, but also in the design, fit, and overall shape of the aircraft. The inner surfaces of the paired wing elevons are well finished. These elevons combine the functions of elevators and ailerons in controlling the aircraft's pitch (side-to-side) and roll (lengthwise) movement. (Jim Goodall)

Attention to detail is one of the key elements in designing LO aircraft. There are no exposed or unfinished areas along the F-117A's starboard wing. This includes the edges of the elevons and the inboard edges of the wing openings, which are all sealed and finished. A retractable green navigation light is mounted near the wingtip; a red light appears on the port wing. (Jim Goodall)

The inner portion of the elevon-fuselage mating area is covered with RAM. This lack of an opening in this area was another area of LO detail attended to by the F-117A's designers. The mating area is immediately outboard of the 'platypus' engine exhaust duct. The elevons droop down to their full lowered position when the aircraft's hydraulic liquid has 'bled off' from the control surfaces after engine shutdown (Jim Goodall)

Both starboard elevons are lowered on this displayed F-117A. The elevons have an aluminum-skinned metal frame structure, with composite trailing edges. The surface is covered with RAM (Radar Absorbent Material) and painted with Flat Black (FS37038) 'iron ball' paint. This paint dilutes radar waves and was also used on Lockheed's earlier U-2 and SR-71 strategic reconnaissance aircraft. (Jim Goodall)

The only items protruding from the F-117A's undersurface – apart from the main landing gear door – are the four diamond-shaped shock pads placed on the outboard end of each weapons bay door. These pads prevent damage to the fast acting doors when they are opened during flight. The Nighthawk's undersurface is otherwise flat, curving up to the 'platypus' exhaust duct at the trailing edge. (Jim Goodall)

The elevon-fuselage mating area is faceted to match the wing's surface. The line parallel to the elevon's trailing edge separates the composite trailing edge area from the metal-framed portion of this control surface. The F-117A's wings use composite leading and trailing edges, which offer reduced weight over metal surfaces and aid with the aircraft's low Radar Cross Section (RCS). (Jim Goodall)

The elevons on both the port and starboard wings act in unison as elevators for pitch (up and down) control and separately as ailerons for roll control. The F-117A's elevons have a deflection range of +/-60°. The edges of the elevons are faceted as a RCS reduction factor. Inboard of the port inner elevon is the old-style radar reflector, which was attached to the aircraft's jack point. (Jim Goodall)

The F-117A's wing undersurface is faceted approximately halfway along its chord (width) to improve the aircraft's Low Observable (LO) characteristics. The 67.5° wing sweep angle along the leading edge also dissipated radar energy directed at the Nighthawk. Recessed navigation lights – red to port, green to starboard – are fitted to the F-117A's outer wing surfaces, beside the wingtip. (Tony Landis)

The red anti-collision light is placed in the center of the F-117A's port wing on both the lower and upper surfaces. A green formation light fitted to the starboard wing is diamond-shaped – like the other lights placed on the Nighthawk's external surface – to deflect radar waves. (Tony Landis)

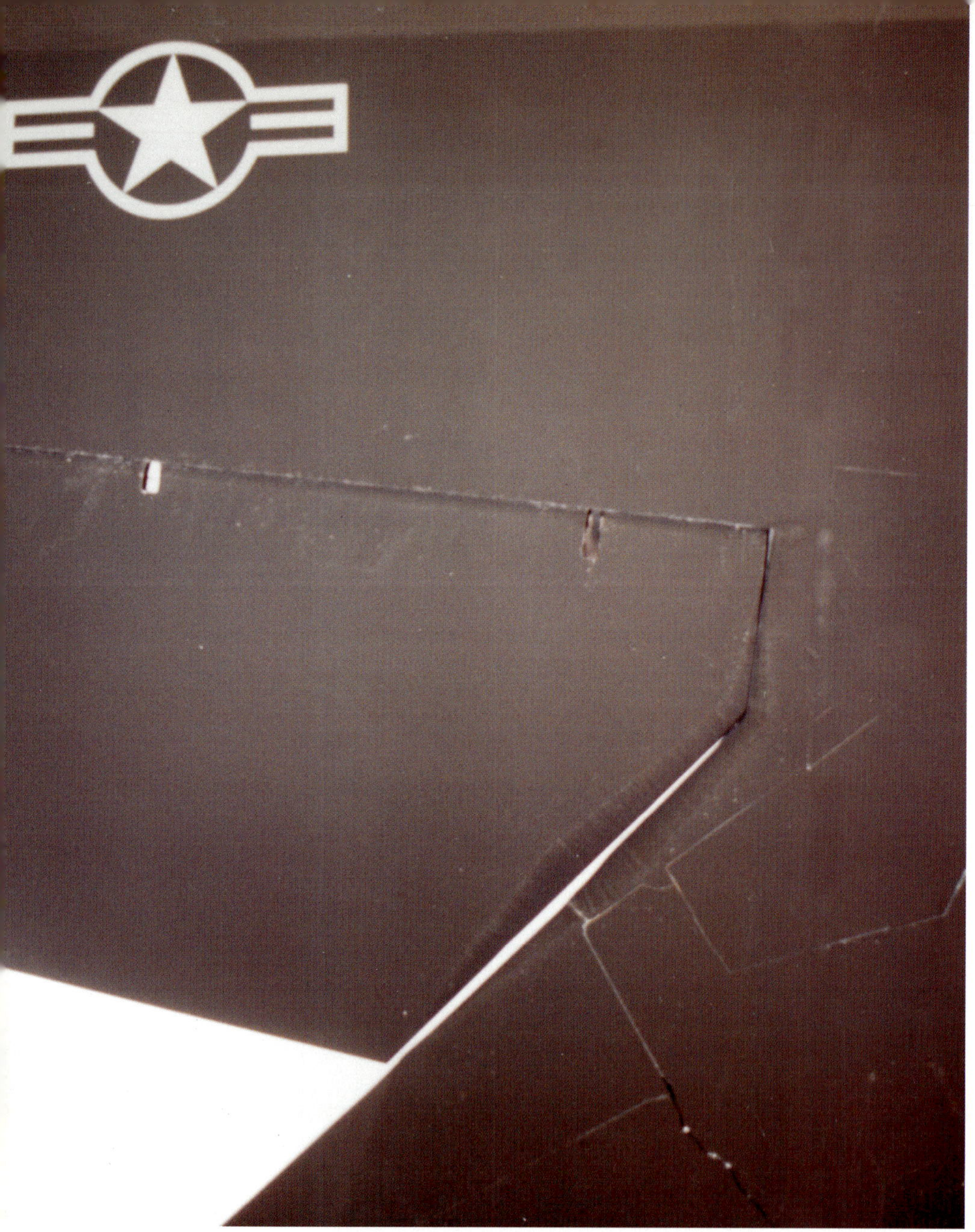

The YF-117A on display at the US Air Force Museum – located at Wright-Patterson Air Force Base, Ohio – is virtually identical in construction to production Nighthawks. This aircraft demonstrates the type of construction and attention to detail lying underneath the RAM covering the F-117As in service. The gap between the inboard elevon and the starboard fuselage is a mere one-half inch. (Jim Goodall)

The F-117A's engine exhaust duct (platypus) is fitted with reddish-colored guide vanes. These vanes maintain thrust direction for the engine exhaust passing through this area and out of the aircraft. The exhaust ejection is covered with ceramic heat tiles able to withstand the hot exhaust gases. The upswept lower lip hides exhaust heat from sensors below the F-117A. (Jim Goodall)

The gap between the inboard elevons where they meet the fuselage is only one-half to three-quarters of an inch (1.3 to 1.9 CM). The elevons are hinged at their leading edge, where they meet the wing. The wing hinges – left open on conventional aircraft – were coated with Radar Absorbent Material (RAM). The fit and finish of the F-117A and other LO (Low Observable) or stealth aircraft is one of the key factors in keeping radar signature down to a minimum. (Jim Goodall)

The F-117A is powered by two 10,800 lb thrust General Electric F404-GE-F1D2 turbofan engines. This powerplant – minus the afterburner – is essentially the same engine used to power the F/A-18 Hornet multi-role fighter. The compressor fan at the front brings air from the engine intake to the combustion chamber, where air and fuel are ignited. The F404-GE-F1D2 has a maximum diameter of 34.8 inches (88.4 CM) and weighs 1730 lbs (784.7 KG). (General Electric via Lockheed Martin)

The starboard General Electric F404 engine was removed from this YF-117A (79-10781) on display at the Air Force Museum. The engine was normally mounted at the aft end of the intake area, which would be kept clean of any loose items that could cause Foreign Object Damage (FOD) to the engine. The inner cavity walls are aft of the intake suction relief door, which was mounted just behind the engine inlet. (Jim Goodall)

A 416th Tactical Fighter Squadron F-117A (85-0830) taxis after landing at Nellis AFB, Nevada on 1 April 1991. Both intake suction relief doors are opened above and aft of the main engine intakes, which was normal for engine start and taxiing. The small white rods just behind the canopy are the Nighthawk's right and left ILS (Instrument Landing System) localizer antennas. Aircraft 830, nicknamed BLACK ASSASSIN, flew 31 missions over Iraq during Operation DESERT STORM before returning stateside. (Jim Goodall)

The narrow engine exhaust ducts not only reduce the F-117A's infrared signature, but also deflect any radar returns at the aft engine assembly. The sloped aft fuselage is broken only by the twin vertical tail surfaces. The F-117A (84-0828) assigned to the Commander of the 37th Tactical Fighter Wing (TFW) was displayed at Nellis AFB, Nevada on 21 April 1990 – the Nighthawk's public debut. (Jim Goodall)

The F-117A's exhaust duct is unique to the Nighthawk family and was one of the features to make this aircraft a Low Observable (LO) design. The narrow exhaust duct and the upswept lower lip explain why this section is correctly termed the 'platypus,' after the duck-billed creature native to Australia. This area was the single hardest item for Lockheed engineers to develop on the F-117A, due to the balance required between performance and LO qualities. (Jim Goodall)

The F-117A's exhaust ducts and adjoining aft fuselage were built with titanium, which has greater heat resistance than aluminum. The exhaust slot measures approximately five feet (1.5 M) wide by six inches (15.2 CM) deep. Each of the 12 grated openings in the exhaust duct measured approximately six square inches (38.7 CM²). Hot jet exhaust gases are cooled with engine bypass air before passing through the exhaust duct. (Jim Goodall)

The heat resistant tiles were removed from the exhaust lip on the Air Force Museum's YF-117A. These tiles – similar to those fitted to the Space Shuttle – protected the metal structure from the engine exhaust heat. High temperature-induced fatigue problems with the exhaust assembly occurred early in the Nighthawk's service career. These problems were corrected in 1991 through improved thermal protection and airflow paths. (Jim Goodall)

The upturned lower intake lip hides the F-117A's exhaust ducts from visual detection when the enemy is just below and aft of the aircraft. This lip also helps shield the Nighthawk's engine and exhaust assembly from Infra-Red and radar detection from behind the F-117A. The two F404-GE-F1D2 engines are easily accessed through large undersurface doors between the weapons bay and main landing gears. (USAF via G. Phillips)

The F-117A's twin tail assembly shields the aircraft's exhaust ducts from viewing from above. The tail consists of two ruddervators (combination rudders and elevators), which operate either in unison for pitch control or separately for yaw control. There is no smooth fairing for the base of the tail surfaces to the aft fuselage. The F-117A's brake parachute is housed at the base of the aircraft's tail, covered by two outboard-hinged doors. (Jim Goodall)

Landing after a mission during Operation DESERT STORM in early 1991, an F-117A deploys its Pioneer Aerospace braking parachute. This ring-type parachute reduces wear on the Nighthawk's brakes as the aircraft slows down from a 172 MPH (276.8 KMH) landing. F-117A brake parachutes are usually black, although white and green 'chutes are sometimes used. Improved carbon-carbon wheel brakes may soon eliminate the need for a brake parachute. (USAF via G. Phillips)

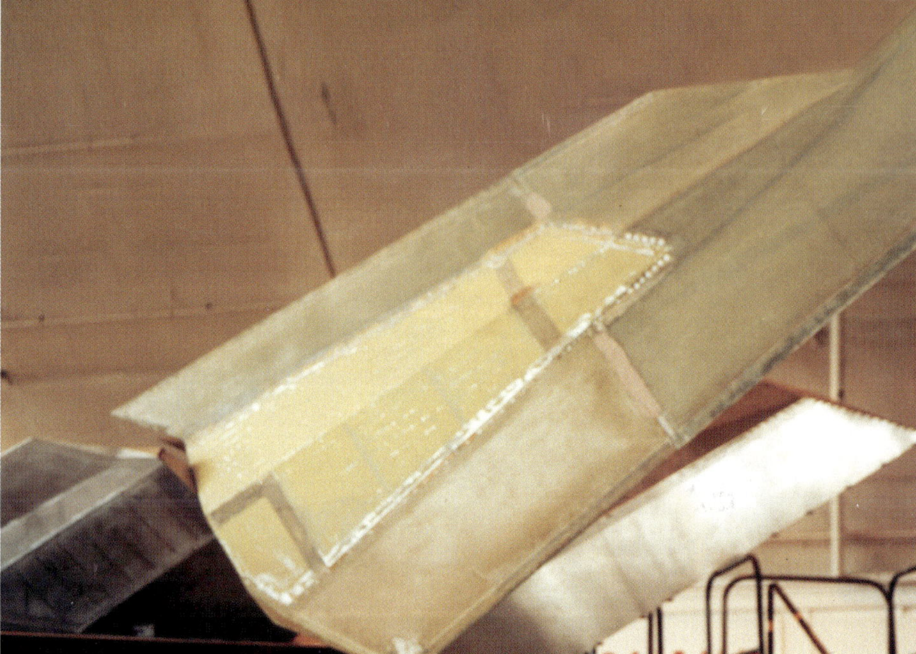

When the second YF-117A (79-10781) was delivered to the US Air Force Museum, the aircraft underwent a sanitation process before the Nighthawk went on public display. The classified Radar Absorbing Material (RAM) and other equipment were removed from the aircraft. The ruddervators lost the RAM, which covered their metal-skinned structure. The YF-117A's exterior was repainted black after the RAM was removed. (Tom Tulus)

F-117A ruddervators are decorated only on their outboard surfaces, which usually includes lettering and insignia in Light Gray (approximately FS36495). Nighthawk 819 (85-0819) was assigned to the Commander of the 49th Fighter Wing (FW) at Holloman Air Force Base, New Mexico. The insignia of the Air Combat Command (ACC) was placed on the upper ruddervator surface. This Nighthawk was named *Raven Beauty* and flew 30 combat missions during Operation DESERT STORM. (Jim Goodall)

There is only a slight space separating the bottoms of the F-117A's ruddervators with the tops of the fixed lower tail portions. These inner surfaces are faceted to deflect radar energy from the aircraft. The rearmost portion of the fuselage is angled to a point between the tail surfaces, also in the interest of lowering the aircraft's Radar Cross Section (RCS). Immediately ahead of the tail surfaces is the braking parachute compartment doors. (Jim Goodall)

Both ruddervators on this 415th Tactical Fighter Squadron (TFS) F-117A (80-0790) were turned slightly to starboard. These surfaces act as rudders when turned in unison. The top of the fixed fin section supporting the ruddervators is faceted and covered to deflect radar waves directed at it. This Nighthawk was named DEADLY JESTER and flew 30 combat missions during Operation DESERT STORM. (Jim Goodall)

These ruddervators are turned facing each other in the role of elevators for the F-117A, as if to point the aircraft's nose up. The tail surfaces are faceted as part of the aircraft's over-all Radar Cross Section (RCS) reduction scheme. Structural material differences account for the different shades of black seen on the ruddervators of this 49th FW Nighthawk. (Kevin Helm)

Two flush-mounted fuel vents are placed in the aft fuselage of the first YF-117A (79-10780), now displayed at the Nellis AFB airpark in Nevada. These vents flank the ridge dividing the port and starboard fuselage undersurfaces and are used to dump excess fuel from the aircraft when required. The Nighthawk's twin tails are angled out in a 'vee' configuration, instead of being angled inward in the case of the HAVE BLUE. (This is the view that would have been seen from Baghdad, Iraq, during DESERT STORM.) (Jim Goodall)

(Above Left) The F-117A's twin 'vee' tail surfaces were adopted because they offered a lower Radar Cross Section (RCS) than the conventional arrangement of a single vertical tail surface and twin horizontal surfaces. The tail surfaces are swept back at 20˚. The Nighthawk's entire exterior surface is covered with smooth, faceted surfaces. These measures aid in reducing the F-117A's frontal RCS to 0.1 square feet (0.009 M^2). The Flat Black (FS37038) paint applied to all Nighthawks is the 'Iron Ball' type also used on Lockheed's U-2/TR-1 and A-12/SR-71 families of strategic reconnaissance aircraft. This paint absorbs and dilutes the radar energy directed at the aircraft. (Jim Goodall)

(Above) The top of the F-117A's fixed fin section is faceted to match the bottom ruddervator surface, yet allowing the ruddervator to deflect up to 30˚ to either port or starboard. The layered Radar Absorbent Material (RAM) resulted in slight ridges in the Nighthawk's exterior finish. The F-117A's original RAM added approximately 2000 pounds (907.2 KG) to the aircraft's weight and required considerable maintenance attention. A new RAM – developed for the Northrop B-2 Spirit stealth bomber and the Lockheed Martin F-22 Raptor fighter – weighs approximately 400 pounds (181.4 KG) and is less maintenance-intensive. The non-standard tail markings on 80-0790 indicate this F-117A's assignments to the commander of the 415th Tactical Fighter Squadron (TFS) and its Aircraft Maintenance Unit (AMU). An AMU performs unit level maintenance on a squadron's aircraft. (Jim Goodall)

(Left) The base of the F-117A's twin 'vee' tail intersects the aft fuselage at right angles. The trailing edges of the fixed fin sections are angled inward. The two drag chute doors are installed just forward of the 'vee' tails on either side of the fuselage centerline. Nighthawks were originally fitted with all-metal ruddervators; however, these units failed once in flight and suffered several near-failures. New graphite thermoplastic ruddervators were installed on the last few production F-117As and retrofitted to earlier aircraft from June of 1990 until August of 1994. (Jim Goodall)

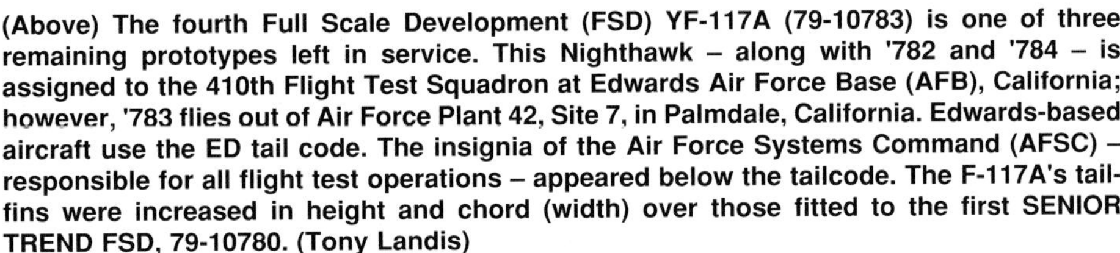

(Above) The fourth Full Scale Development (FSD) YF-117A (79-10783) is one of three remaining prototypes left in service. This Nighthawk – along with '782 and '784 – is assigned to the 410th Flight Test Squadron at Edwards Air Force Base (AFB), California; however, '783 flies out of Air Force Plant 42, Site 7, in Palmdale, California. Edwards-based aircraft use the ED tail code. The insignia of the Air Force Systems Command (AFSC) – responsible for all flight test operations – appeared below the tailcode. The F-117A's tail-fins were increased in height and chord (width) over those fitted to the first SENIOR TREND FSD, 79-10780. (Tony Landis)

(Above Right) The Commander of the 37th Tactical Fighter Wing (TFW) had non-standard markings applied to the tail of his F-117A (84-0828). The TR tail code represented Tonopah Test Range in western Nevada, 140 miles (225.3 KM) northwest of Las Vegas. The Tactical Air Command (TAC) emblem was painted in light gray outline on the upper ruddervator. This unit was originally called the 4450th Test Group (TG) when it was sent from Groom Dry Lake (Area 51) to Tonopah in 1982. This Group was redesignated the 37th TFW on 5 October 1989 – 11 months after the Pentagon publicly revealed the existence of the F-117A. (Nick Waters)

(Right) Nighthawks of the 37th TFW display a variety of tail markings upon their arrival at Nellis AFB, Nevada on 1 April 1991, following Operation DESERT STORM. At least two F-117As display the TR tailcode for their home base of Tonopah Test Range, while the remainder do not have these letters. All aircraft display the last three digits of their serial number under USAF on the lower ruddervator surfaces. Aircraft 810 has an outline stencil version of the TAC insignia, while the other Nighthawks have low-visibility TAC emblems applied in three shades of gray. (Jim Goodall)

This F-117A (82-0804) was assigned to Detachment 1, 57th Wing at Holloman AFB, New Mexico. This unit performs testing and evaluation of F-117A tactics and weapons for possible later use by operational Nighthawk units. The WA tailcode is assigned to the Weapons and Tactics Center (WTC) – parent to the 57th Wing – at Nellis AFB, Nevada. The tailband on the ruddervator is a two-tone gray checkerboard, a low-visibility version of the Wing's traditional black and yellow checkerboard tailband. The insignia of Air Combat Command (ACC) – which superceded TAC and Strategic Air Command (SAC) on 1 June 1992 – was placed under the tailband. The ACC insignia is exactly the same as for TAC, except for the wording AIR COMBAT COMMAND on the bottom. (Paul Crickmore Collection)

The 49th Fighter Wing Commander's F-117A, (82-0803) displays the insignia of its three flying units on a light gray tailband. Insignia represent (from front): the 7th Combat Training Squadron (CTS) 'Bunyaps/Screamin' Demons,' which serves as the F-117A Replacement Training Unit; the 8th Fighter Squadron (FS) 'Black Sheep'; and the 9th FS 'Iron Knights.' All three Squadrons are based together at Holloman AFB. Nighthawk 803 carried the name UNEXPECTED GUEST and completed 33 combat missions over Baghdad during Operation DESERT STORM in early 1991. (Paul Crickmore)

49th Fighter Wing/Operations Group Insignia

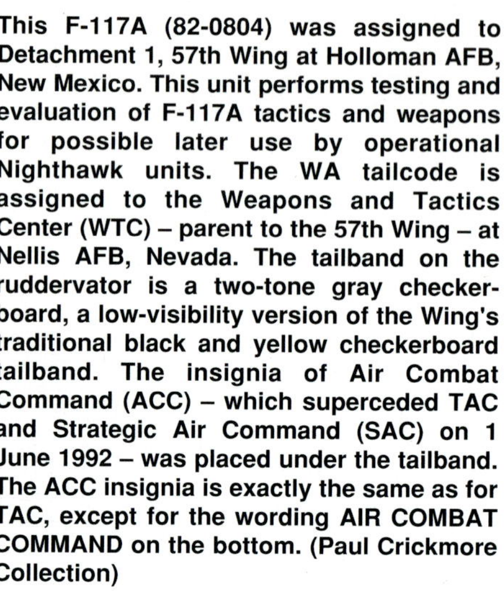

7th Fighter Squadron (FS) Insignia

8th FS Insignia

9th FS Insignia

At one point, the 49th FW's Commander was assigned another F-117A, 85-0816. This Nighthawk also displayed the insignia of the Wing's three squadrons on the tailband, while the lettering was in two shades of gray. (Brian C. Rogers)

This F-117A (85-0819) also served as the 49th FW Commander's aircraft; however, this Nighthawk had 'Plain Jane' markings. The lettering was Light Gray (approximately FS 36495) on the Flat Black (FS37038) surface, with the ACC insignia on the upper tail. (Jim Goodall)

This F-117A (82-0806) was assigned to the 9th FS, 49th FW and carried FLYING KNIGHTS on the red outlined tail band. This Nighthawk was lost over Serbia on 28 March 1999 – the first combat loss of the F-117A. The pilot safely ejected and was rescued. (Brian C. Rogers)

This Nighthawk (85-0829) is decorated with the black and yellow tailband of the 9th FS, the 'Black Sheep.' The Squadron is assigned to the 49th FW at Holloman AFB. (Greg L. Davis)

F-117A 85-0816 displays a white tailband with a black pitchfork and SCREAMIN DEMONS legend. This aircraft was assigned to the 7th CTS, 49th FW, which trains new F-117A crews. (Brian C. Rogers)

This F-117A (84-0809) was assigned to the 49th FW; however, there is no indication of squadron identity on the tail. The multi-gray low-visibility version of the ACC insignia was painted on the ruddervator's upper surface. (Brian C. Rogers)

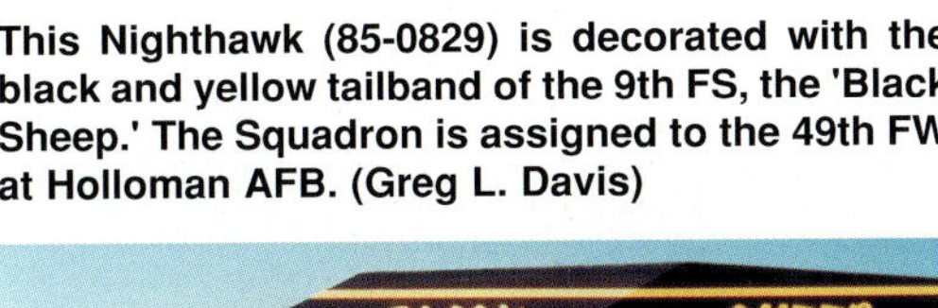

This F-117A (85-0819) made one of the first public appearances of an HO-coded F-117A and an early display of the FW code designating Fighter Wing. This is a superbly clean aircraft, as required by Air Force and ACC Headquarters for aircraft participating in air shows. Nighthawks have usually displayed only the last three digits of their serial number and did not display the two-digit Fiscal Year (FY) preface normally found on US Air Force aircraft. (Jim Goodall)

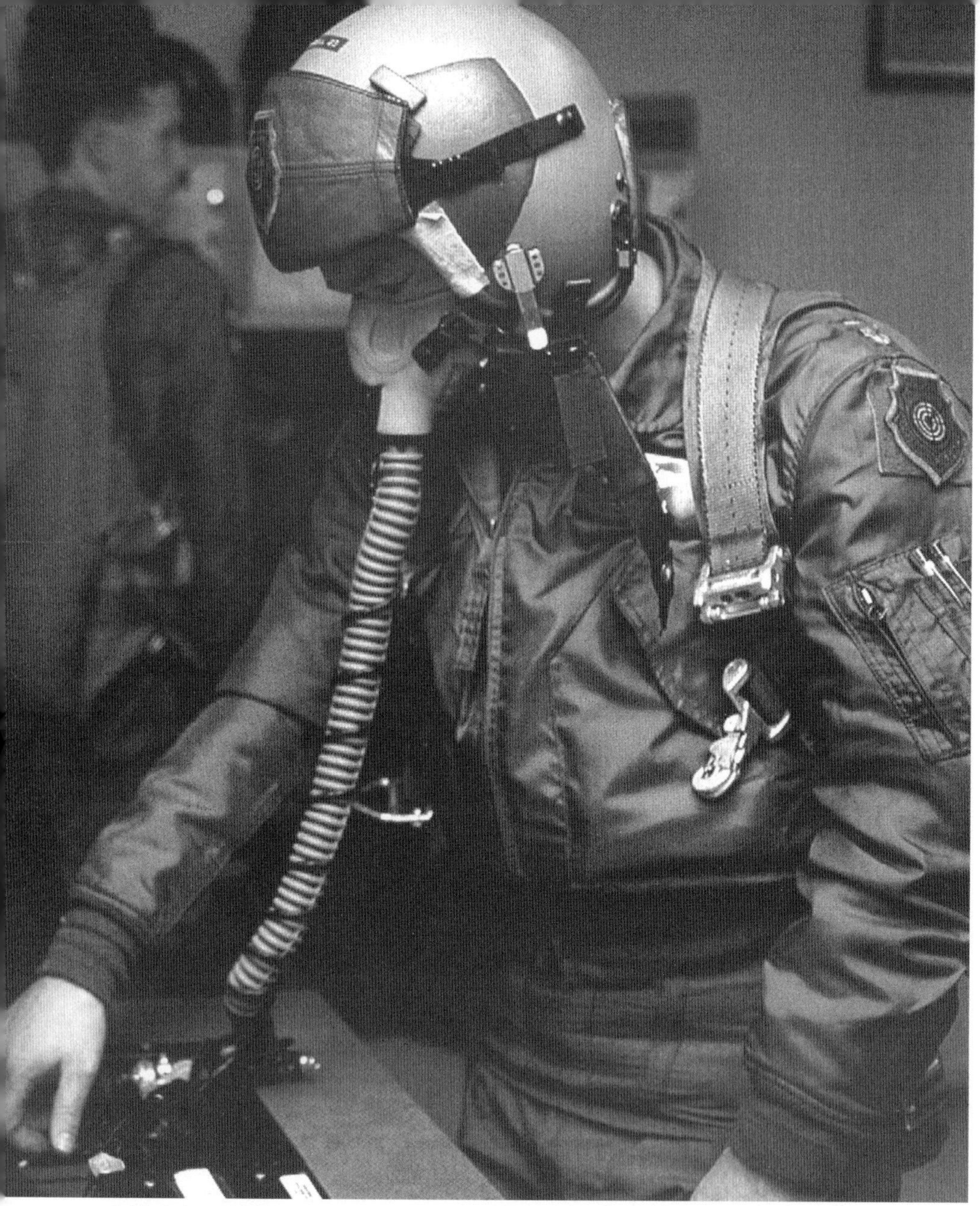

Two F-117A pilots of the 417th Tactical Fighter Training Squadron (TFTS) zip up their partial G suits prior to a flight. These G suits are a standard issue requirement for all service pilots and worn over the olive green flight suit. During high G (force of gravity) maneuvers, air bladders in the G suit inflate to exert pressure on the pilot's abdomen and legs. This action prevents blood from pooling below his chest, which can result in the pilot 'blacking out' (losing consciousness). (Lockheed Martin)

Maj Joe Bowley of the 415th Tactical Fighter Squadron, 37th TFW prepares for takeoff in his F-117A from Saudi Arabia following Operation DESERT STORM in early 1991. He wore a black helmet, which was sometimes chosen by F-117A pilots, although most pilots used the standard issue gray helmets. The shoulder harness on the ACES II ejection seat allows the pilot some forward movement within the cockpit, yet secures him back into the seat during ejection. (USAF via G. Phillips)

A Nighthawk pilot assigned to the 37th TFW at Tonopah Test Range performs an oxygen mask check prior to leaving the operations center for the flight line. The oxygen hose is plugged into the test unit and air is run through the hose to ensure airflow into the oxygen mask. This F-117A pilot's jacket has the 57th Fighter Weapons Wing (now 57th Wing) insignia on a Velcro left upper sleeve patch. This patch allows the unit insignia to be removed on combat missions, which reduced intelligence information to the enemy should the pilot be captured. (Lockheed Martin)

Maj Bowley performs a pre-flight inspection on his F-117A prior to departing Saudi Arabia for the US following Operation DESERT STORM. The hose connected to the nose landing gear well sends compressed air to the two engines' starters. The red REMOVE BEFORE FLIGHT tag is attached to the retraction strut lock, which will be removed by the crew chief prior to engine start. (USAF via G. Phillips)

Staff Sgt David Owings adjusts the shoulder harness straps securing Maj Bowley into the seat of this F-117A just after the 1991 Persian Gulf War. Owings served as the crew chief for this Nighthawk and was responsible for maintaining the aircraft for each mission. Two other enlisted crewmen usually assisted F-117A crew chiefs in performing routine maintenance on each aircraft. (USAF via G. Phillips)

A 49th FW F-117A releases 2000 pound (907.2 KG) GBU-27 Laser Guided Bombs (LGBs) over the Nellis Bombing Range in Nevada. The two weapons – painted with white stripes for improved tracking by observers – are released 1.5 seconds apart to allow proper separation. The retractable tail fins have extended 50% on the lower GBU-27, but have not yet extended on the second bomb released. Both the GBU-27 (also called the BLU-109) and the GBU-10 LGBs can hit a 3.3 ft (1 M) target at night from 25,000 feet (7620 M) altitude – not bad for such an 'ugly' aircraft! (Lockheed Martin)

The undersurface of the third YF-117A Full Scale Development (FSD) aircraft (79-10782) was painted to resemble an American flag on 14 December 1983. This scheme was applied for a change of command ceremony at Area 51 (Groom Dry Lake), Nevada. Paul Tackabury replaced Roger Moseley as commander of Detachment 5, Air Force Flight Test Center (AFFTC), while Jon Beesley made a flyby in the specially decorated 782 during the ceremony. (Lockheed Martin)

The 4450th Tactical Group (TG) was the original US Air Force unit to operate the F-117A. This Group flew the Nighthawk from Tonopah Test Range from 1981 until 5 October 1989, when the 4450th TG was redesignated the 37th Tactical Fighter Wing.

The 4450th Test Squadron (TS) of the 4450th TG was the F-117A Replacement Training Unit (RTU). The 'Goat Suckers' flew Vought A-7D Corsair IIs for proficiency flights and as a cover for the secret Nighthawk operations.

The 4450th TS 'Nightstalkers' was activated under the 4450th TG on 11 June 1981. This Squadron flew F-117As from late 1982 until deactivated on 5 October 1989.

The 4453rd Test and Evaluation Squadron (T&ES) 'Grim Reapers' of the 4450th TG flew T-38 Talons on chase flights alongside the F-117As. This Squadron also conducted area familiarization flights for the Group. The 4453rd T&ES became the 417th Tactical Fighter Squadron on 5 October 1989.

A 37th TFW F-117A with its landing gear extended is accompanied by a Northrop AT-38B Talon as it crosses the Tonopah Test Range's perimeter fence during the summer of 1989. AT-38Bs were assigned to Nighthawk units to provide continuation training for pilots and for instructors to fly chase with new F-117A pilots making their early flights in this aircraft. This photograph was the first civilian image captured of the F-117A – nearly one year before the Nighthawk's initial public display at Nellis AFB on 21 April 1990. (Tony Landis)

Pete's Dragon – a character from a Walt Disney movie – was the nickname given to the second operational F-117A (80-0787) assigned to the USAF's Tactical Air Command (TAC). This patch was designed for Pete Barnes – the second operational F-117A pilot in TAC – to wear on his flightsuit. Barnes flew Nighthawk 787 for the first time on 9 July 1982.

This patch was given to Lockheed personnel assigned to F-117A flight test operations.

This patch was issued to Lockheed Depot Field Maintenance Team personnel assigned to the HAVE BLUE project.

This unofficial insignia expresses the qualities of the F-117A Nighthawk and its personnel.

Lockheed Field Service Representatives and 37th TFW personnel sent to Saudi Arabia for Operation DESERT STORM in early 1991 were given this patch.

F-117A 810 (84-0810) undergoes depot level maintenance at Site 7 of Air Force Plant 42 in Palmdale, California. Site 7 – also called PS77 – is the Lockheed Martin/Air Force overhaul facility for the Nighthawk. Workers have removed the engine inlet assembly, the canopy, the ejection seat, and most of the cockpit from this Nighthawk. This step preceded the OCIP (Offensive Capability Improvement Program) Phase 3 upgrade of the cockpit and IRAD (Infra-Red Acquisition and Detection) system. (Lockheed Martin)

Lockheed delivered the 59th and final F-117A to the Air Force in a ceremony at the new Skunk Works facility at Air Force Plant 42, Site 10 in Palmdale on 12 July 1990. This Nighthawk (88-0843) was assigned to the 415th Tactical Fighter Squadron (TFS), 37th TFW at Tonopah Test Range. The aircraft was nicknamed AFFECTIONATELY CHRISTINE and flew 33 combat missions against Iraq during the 1991 Persian Gulf War. (Tony Landis)

An F-117A assigned to the commander of the 37th Tactical Fighter Wing (TFW) taxis at Nellis Air Force Base (AFB), Nevada on 21 April 1990, when the Nighthawk was publicly viewed for the first time. Parked in the background are several Fairchild Republic A-10A Thunderbolt II (Warthog) and McDonnell Douglas F-15E Eagle aircraft. The A-10 and the F-15, like the F-117A, would all see action less than one year later over Iraq and Kuwait during Operation DESERT STORM. (Jim Goodall)

Ground crews attend to 22 Nighthawks of the 37th TFW at Langley AFB, Virginia on 19 August 1990, after the F-117As arrived from Tonopah. Eighteen of these aircraft departed from Langley the next day for Saudi Arabia during Operation DESERT SHIELD, the US-led defensive action following Iraq's invasion of Kuwait on 2 August 1990. Replacement brake parachutes will be fitted to the open aft fuselage compartment doors. (USAF via G. Phillips)

A refueling boom is connected to a 37th TFW F-117A's receptacle during the deployment to Saudi Arabia on 20 August 1990. Each Nighthawk required four to six aerial refuelings to cover the 15-hour flight from Langley AFB, Virginia to King Khalid Air Base (AB), near Khamis Mushait, Saudi Arabia. The F-117A's eight fuel tanks have a total capacity of approximately 2800 gallons (10,599.2 L) of JP-8 fuel. (USAF via G. Phillips)

Maintenance crewmen service a 37th TFW (Provisional) F-117A beside a hardened shelter at King Khalid AB, Saudi Arabia during Operation Desert Shield. Each reinforced concrete shelter – built under supervision by US Army engineers – housed two Nighthawks. King Khalid was located near Khamis Mushait in southwest Saudi Arabia, 1000 miles (1609.3 KM) from Baghdad, Iraq. The 37th TFW (P) had 42 F-117As available when Operation DESERT STORM began on 17 January 1991. (USAF via G. Phillips)

A Nighthawk assigned to the 37th TFW (P) sits inside its hardened shelter at King Khalid AB during Operation DESERT SHIELD. An earthing wire connected the F-117A's port wing to the concrete floor; this wire dissipated static electrical charges, which could damage the aircraft's delicate electronic systems. Each hardened shelter at King Khalid had openings at opposite sides, allowing an aircraft to taxi through in either direction. (USAF via G. Phillips)

A 37th Aircraft Maintenance Unit (AMU) technician performs routine maintenance on an F-117A in the hangar revetment area at King Khalid AB, Saudi Arabia. This maintenance was performed during a lull in sorties over Baghdad during Operation DESERT STORM. The Nighthawk's distinctive crew access ladder skirts the aircraft's faceted surface and protected the F-117A's Radar Absorbent Material (RAM) from damage. (Lockheed Martin)

A 37th TFW F-117A (83-0807) is parked on the ramp at Tonopah Test Range (TTR), Nevada. Another Nighthawk is positioned to 807's port rear quarter. The Wing's insignia is painted in low-visibility style on the F-117A's forward fuselage, between the intake grill and the national insignia. Nighthawk 807 was nicknamed THE CHICKENHAWK when it flew 14 DESERT STORM combat missions for the Wing's 415th TFS. Personnel assigned to the 37th TFW – except for base security – commuted weekly by air from Nellis Air Force Base (AFB), Nevada to TTR, a 190 mile (305.8 KM) one-way trip. These flights were carried out by civilian contractors for the USAF. (Lockheed Martin)

This F-117A (85-0816) assigned to the commander of the 7th Fighter Squadron (FS), 49th FW flies over the Nighthawk hangars at Holloman AFB, New Mexico. Two 'Black Jets' are housed in each specially-built hangar on the base, located eight miles (12.9 KM) southeast of Alamogordo, NM. Buildings across from the hangars housed various support functions and equipment associated with the aircraft. The 49th FW replaced their F-15C Eagles with the 37th TFW's F-117As from April of 1992. Nighthawk 816 was called LONE WOLF when it flew 30 combat missions against Iraq during the 1991 Persian Gulf War, while assigned to the 415th TFS. (US Air Force via Lockheed Martin)

An F-117A backs away from a tanker aircraft following a mid-air refueling. Spilled JP-8 fuel has stained the area immediately aft of the Nighthawk's refueling receptacle. This receptacle rotates on the aircraft's centerline and is only open during actual air refueling. It is illuminated at night by the light located on the F-117A canopy's peak. Without this light, boom operators on KC-135R or KC-10A tankers would see nothing but total darkness. (Mike Dornheim, AvWeek)

An F-117A ground crew member sits in the cockpit of 84-0825 as it is towed to its hangar at King Khalid Air Base in southwest Saudi Arabia during Operation DESERT STORM. He would use the Nighthawk's brakes as a safety precaution during towing operations. This particular F-117A was called MAD-MAX and flew 33 combat missions during the 1991 Persian Gulf War. A Nighthawk detachment is maintained at King Khalid to help deter further aggression in the Persian Gulf region. (US Air Force)

A 37th TFW (Provisional) F-117A is towed away from a hardened shelter at King Khalid AB during DESERT STORM. The Nighthawk is compatible with standard Air Force ground support equipment, including the tow bar. The aircraft's crew ladder is draped over front of the Clark ground tug. Rocks placed on the shelters' roofs helped camouflage these concrete hangars from aerial view. King Khalid was never attacked during the 1991 Gulf War; however, wartime security was tight. (US Air Force)

Gen H. Norman Schwartzkopf, CINC CENTCOM (Commander-in-Chief, US Central Command), is briefed on the F-117A by a 37th TFW (P) pilot at King Khalid AB during Operation DESERT STORM. Schwartzkopf frequently displayed the results of Nighthawk attacks – recorded by the aircraft's IRAD system – during his wartime press briefings in Riyadh, Saudi Arabia. (US Air Force)

Two Nighthawks are parked in tandem inside one of King Khalid's hardened shelters during Operation DESERT SHIELD. These shelters protected the aircraft from possible enemy attack and from the harsh desert climate. The F-117As deployed to Saudi Arabia represented only 2.5% of all Coalition combat aircraft in the Gulf region; however, they attacked over 40% of the strategic military targets in Iraq. (USAF via G. Phillips)

The first Full Scale Development (FSD) YF-117A (79-10780) was nicknamed 'Scorpion 1' and first flew on 18 June 1981. The SENIOR TREND aircraft was nicknamed the 'Baja Scorpion' by ground crewmen due to its unusual shape. Aircraft 780's canopy bore the names of its test pilots: Skip Anderson, Hal Farley, and Tom Morgenfeld.

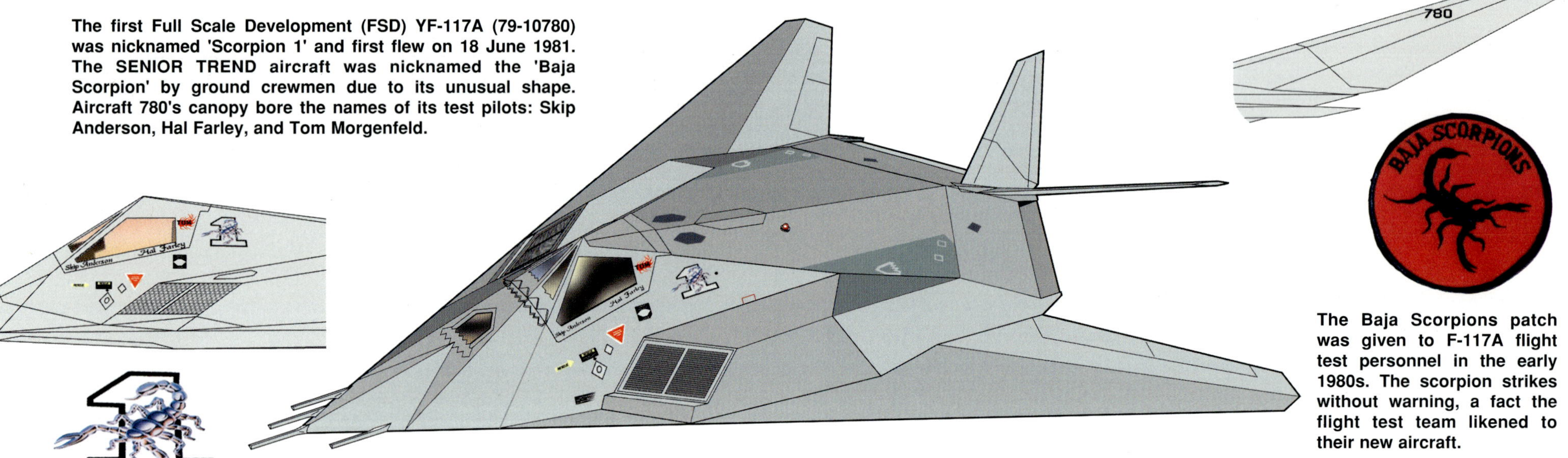

The Baja Scorpions patch was given to F-117A flight test personnel in the early 1980s. The scorpion strikes without warning, a fact the flight test team likened to their new aircraft.

Test pilot Hal Farley flew the first FSD YF-117A (Aircraft 780) over the Nellis Range on 18 June 1981. Although the F-117A (SENIOR TREND) program was kept highly classified, the FSD aircraft flew during daylight hours. The YF-117A was finished in overall Light Gray (approximately FS36375) with no national markings. (Lockheed Martin via Tony Landis)

Lockheed fitted the first FSD YF-117A (780) with leading edge extensions (LEXs) between December of 1983 and February of 1984. These LEXs worked well enough to reduce the aircraft's landing speed by approximately 10 knots (11.5 MPH; 18.5 KMH); however, this improvement was not enough to justify modification of the entire Nighthawk fleet. The port undersurface wingtip was painted orange for improved visibility. (Lockheed Martin via Tony Landis)

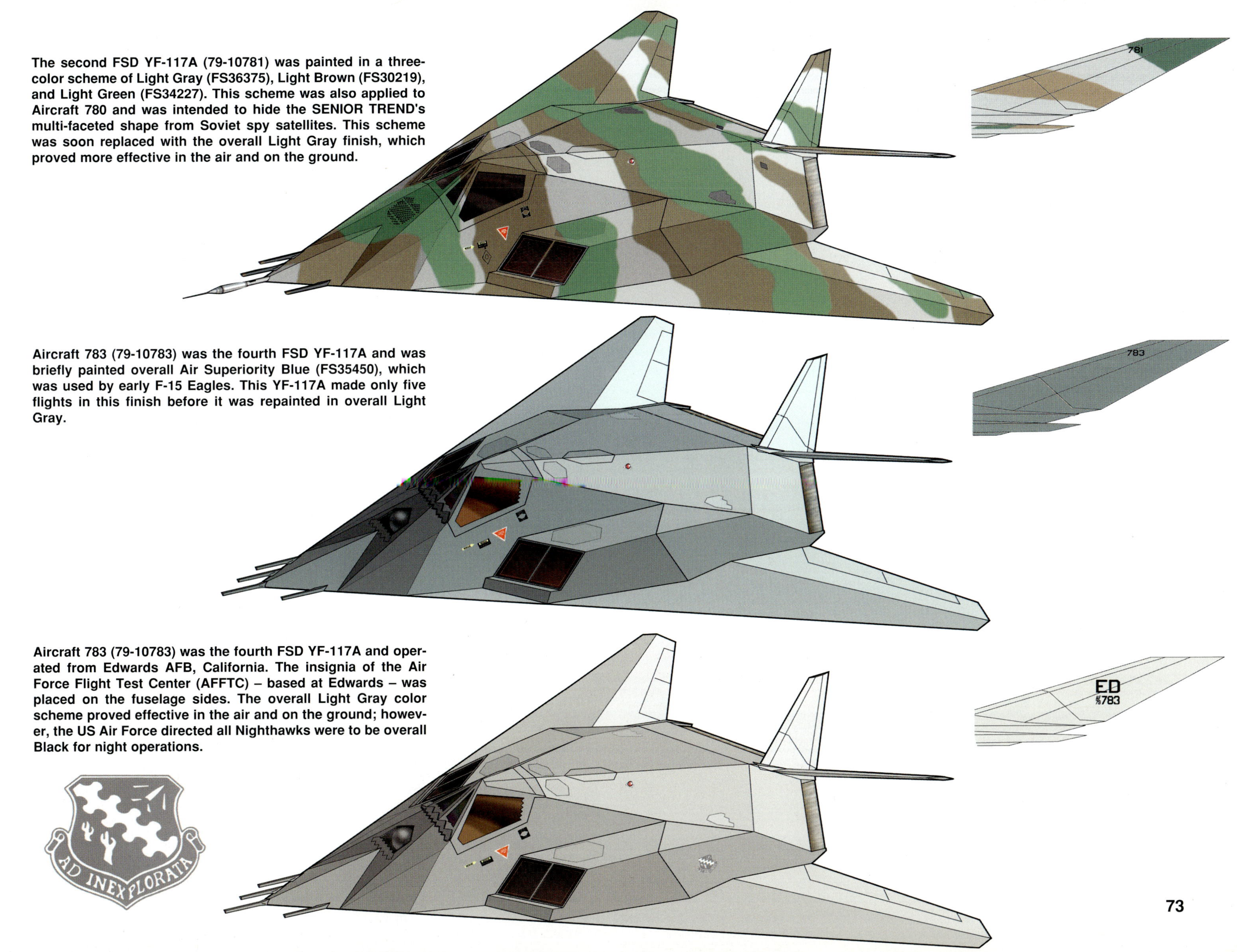

The second FSD YF-117A (79-10781) was painted in a three-color scheme of Light Gray (FS36375), Light Brown (FS30219), and Light Green (FS34227). This scheme was also applied to Aircraft 780 and was intended to hide the SENIOR TREND's multi-faceted shape from Soviet spy satellites. This scheme was soon replaced with the overall Light Gray finish, which proved more effective in the air and on the ground.

Aircraft 783 (79-10783) was the fourth FSD YF-117A and was briefly painted overall Air Superiority Blue (FS35450), which was used by early F-15 Eagles. This YF-117A made only five flights in this finish before it was repainted in overall Light Gray.

Aircraft 783 (79-10783) was the fourth FSD YF-117A and operated from Edwards AFB, California. The insignia of the Air Force Flight Test Center (AFFTC) – based at Edwards – was placed on the fuselage sides. The overall Light Gray color scheme proved effective in the air and on the ground; however, the US Air Force directed all Nighthawks were to be overall Black for night operations.

73

F-117A (84-0810) arrives at Nellis Air Force Base, Nevada in the early afternoon of 21 April 1991. This Nighthawk was the first of eight F-117As to return to the US from King Khalid AB, Saudi Arabia following Operation DESERT STORM. Aircraft 810 – named DARK ANGEL – had 26 combat mission markings painted just below the canopy rail. (Jim Goodall)

Seven F-117A of the 37th TFW are lined up on the Nellis AFB ramp following their triumphant return to American soil on 1 April 1991. These Nighthawks flew from King Khalid AB, Saudi Arabia to Seymour Johnson AFB, North Carolina, where fresh pilots awaited them. The relief pilots checked the aircraft before flying the F-117As to Nellis and a gathering of family, friends, and the press. (Jim Goodall)

Col Al Whitley, Commander of the 37th Tactical Fighter Wing (TFW), taxis his F-117A (85-0813, THE TOXIC AVENGER) at Nellis AFB after arriving on 1 April 1991. This Nighthawk flew 35 missions over Iraq during the Persian Gulf War. The arrival of the 37th TFW's F-117As from Saudi Arabia marked the first time the general public was allowed to see how the weapons doors really opened. (Jim Goodall)

An Air Force security policeman stands before a 37th TFW F-117A on display at the 1991 Paris Air Show. This June event marked the Nighthawk's first public appearance outside the US. Arrayed before the F-117A were two 2000 pound (907.2 KG) GBU-24 Paveway III laser guided bombs. A perimeter fence kept onlookers away from the aircraft's sensitive RAM (Radar Absorbent Material) external surfaces. (USAF via G. Phillips)

The 49th FW commander's F-117A is accompanied by an AT-38B Talon during a new pilot training mission from Holloman AFB, New Mexico. The abbreviation 12 AF under the AT-38B's HO (for Holloman) tailcode stands for the 12th Air Force. This Air Force controls the 49th FW and other Air Combat Command (ACC) assets – apart from bombers and strategic reconnaissance assets – based in the western US. This Talon was painted in three-tone Aggressor blue (FS35109, FS35164, and FS35622). The Wing's AT-38Bs were later repainted overall Gloss Black (FS17038) to match the F-117As. (Lockheed Martin via Greg L. Davis)

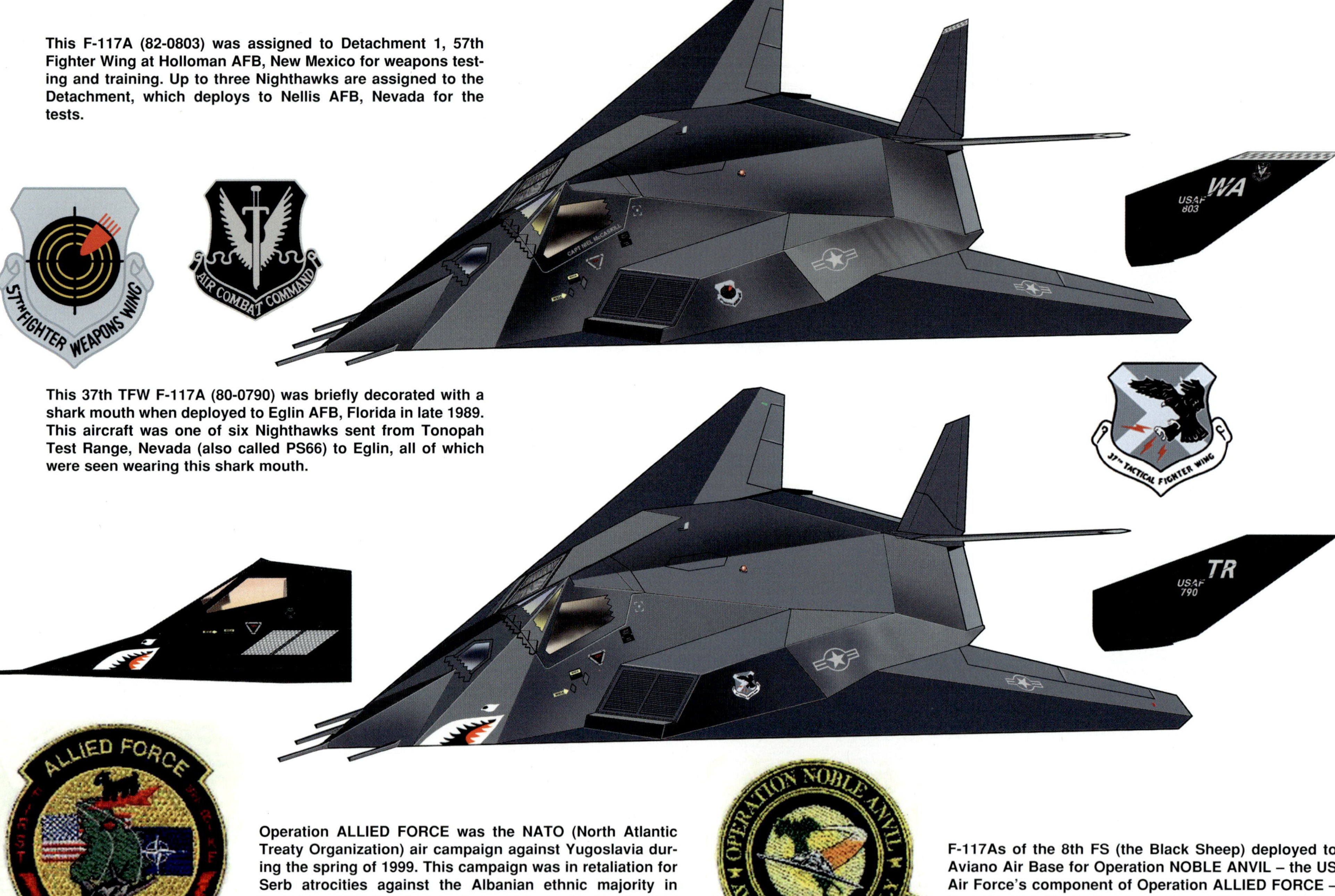

This F-117A (82-0803) was assigned to Detachment 1, 57th Fighter Wing at Holloman AFB, New Mexico for weapons testing and training. Up to three Nighthawks are assigned to the Detachment, which deploys to Nellis AFB, Nevada for the tests.

This 37th TFW F-117A (80-0790) was briefly decorated with a shark mouth when deployed to Eglin AFB, Florida in late 1989. This aircraft was one of six Nighthawks sent from Tonopah Test Range, Nevada (also called PS66) to Eglin, all of which were seen wearing this shark mouth.

Operation ALLIED FORCE was the NATO (North Atlantic Treaty Organization) air campaign against Yugoslavia during the spring of 1999. This campaign was in retaliation for Serb atrocities against the Albanian ethnic majority in Kosovo. F-117As stationed at Aviano Air Base, Italy attacked key Yugoslav targets. The 8th Fighter Squadron lost one of its Nighthawks – apparently to a Serb Surface-to-Air Missile – near Belgrade on 28 March 1999. This was the first combat loss of an F-117A.

F-117As of the 8th FS (the Black Sheep) deployed to Aviano Air Base for Operation NOBLE ANVIL – the US Air Force's component of Operation ALLIED FORCE – in early 1999. The facility in northern Italy served as the base for the Nighthawks and other US aircraft involved in the air assault on Yugoslavia. Following NOBLE ANVIL, the 8th FS returned to Holloman AFB, New Mexico.

This F-117A (85-0816) has the distinction of being the first Nighthawk to drop its bombs in combat. This occurred during Operation JUST CAUSE – the US invasion of Panama – on 19-20 December 1989. Maj Greg Feest led six F-117As in a harassment attack on a field near the Panamanian Defense Force barracks near Ria Hato. Feest – promoted to Lt Col – also flew '816 in dropping the first bomb on Iraq, when Operation DESERT STORM began on 17 January 1991.

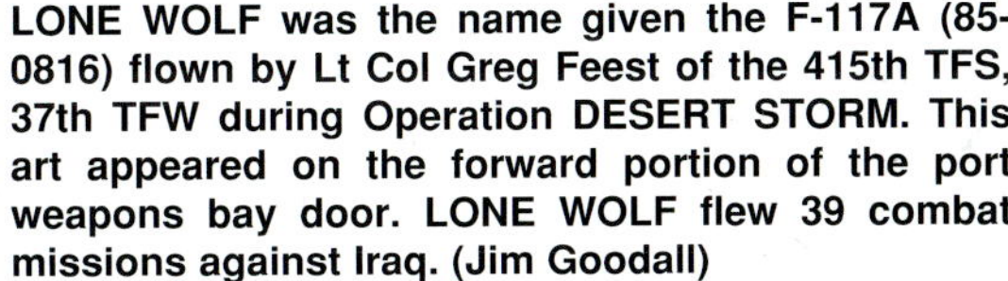

The USAF's Tactical Air Command (TAC) was disbanded on 1 June 1992 and its combat assets – including the F-117As – were combined with the strategic bomber and reconnaissance aircraft of the former Strategic Air Command (SAC) into the new Air Combat Command (ACC).

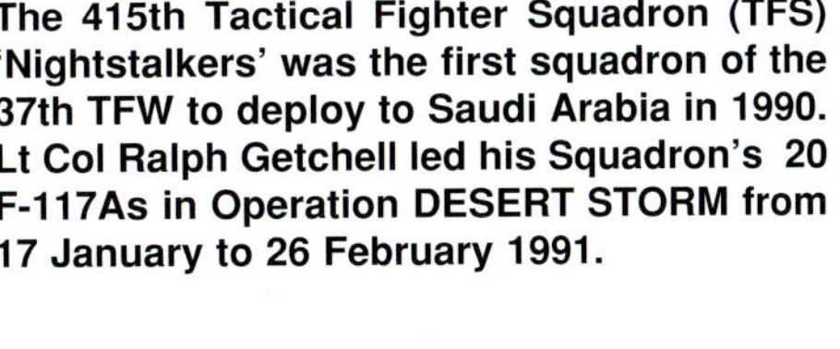

LONE WOLF was the name given the F-117A (85-0816) flown by Lt Col Greg Feest of the 415th TFS, 37th TFW during Operation DESERT STORM. This art appeared on the forward portion of the port weapons bay door. LONE WOLF flew 39 combat missions against Iraq. (Jim Goodall)

An F-117A assigned to the 37th TFW dropped the first bomb of the 1991 Persian Gulf War (Operation DESERT STORM) at 0251 hrs on 17 January 1991. This bomb partially destroyed an Iraqi air defense center at Nukayb, which was soon completely destroyed by a second Nighthawk's bomb. Ten more F-117As attacked Baghdad soon afterward.

The 415th Tactical Fighter Squadron (TFS) 'Nightstalkers' was the first squadron of the 37th TFW to deploy to Saudi Arabia in 1990. Lt Col Ralph Getchell led his Squadron's 20 F-117As in Operation DESERT STORM from 17 January to 26 February 1991.

The 416th TFS 'Ghost Riders' deployed 22 F-117As to Saudi Arabia in December of 1990, reinforcing the 415th TFS already in theatre. Lt Col Gregory Gonyea commanded the Squadron's 22 Nighthawks during Operation DESERT STORM.

The 417th Tactical Fighter Training Squadron (TFTS) 'Bandits' was the 37th TFW's RTU. This Squadron did not deploy to the Persian Gulf for Operation DESERT STORM; however, eight of the 417th TFTS's F-117As were available as attrition replacements. None of these aircraft were needed.

A ground crew member is attaching a grounding wire from a 49th FW F-117A (85-0819) to a terminal on the hangar floor at Holloman AFB. Hangar floors are kept clean by ground crewmen removing anything that could cause Foreign Object Damage (FOD) to the aircraft's engines. The flush mounted white inlet grill illumination light under the canopy sill was turned on. The Wing's insignia was placed on the forward fuselage just aft of the engine inlets. The spring-loaded intake suction relief doors immediately above the engine inlets hang down approximately four to five inches (10.2 to 12.7 CM). These doors close when the Nighthawk is in the air through inlet air pressure. (Tony Landis)

Deployed members of the 8th Fighter Squadron (the 'Black Sheep') pose in front of the 49th Fighter Wing Commander's F-117A at Ahmed Al-Jaber Air Base, Kuwait in 1998. The Squadron's deployment to Kuwait was a part of Operation SOUTHERN WATCH, the US effort to deter further Iraqi aggression in the Persian Gulf region. The Hardened Aircraft Shelter (HAS) in the background was hit during Operation DESERT STORM seven years before, most likely by an F-117A's Laser Guided Bomb. (Greg L. Davis)

An F-117A is readied to back into a bomb resistance shelter at Aviano Air Base, Italy on 21 February 1999. Nighthawks from the 49th FW were deployed to Italy for Operation ALLIED FORCE, the NATO (North Atlantic Treaty Organization) bombing campaign against Yugoslavia. The 25 F-117As sent to Aviano attacked high-priority Yugoslav targets in Serbia and Kosovo. (US Air Force)

This F-117A from the 9th FS, 49th FW displays 25 mission marks representing sorties over Yugoslavia during Operation ALLIED FORCE. The first combat loss of a Nighthawk occurred on 28 March 1999, when 82-0806 was downed – apparently by a Serb surface-to-air missile – approximately 30 miles (48.3 km) northeast of Belgrade, the Yugoslav capital. The F-117A pilot safely ejected and was rescued by a US combat search-and-rescue team. (Kevin Helm)

More DESERT STORM Aircraft

1095 AH-64 Apache in Action

1130 B-52 Stratofortress in Action

5506 B-52 Walk Around

5517 A-10 Warthog Walk Around

5518 F/A-18 Hornet Walk Around

5519 UH-60 Black Hawk Walk Around

from squadron/signal publications